FINANCIAL STATEMENTS

A Crusade for Current Values

Financial Statements

A CRUSADE FOR CURRENT VALUES

Howard Ross, C.A.

Partner in Touche Ross & Co., Canada

PITMAN PUBLISHING CORPORATION

New York • *Toronto* • *London*

To Barney,
who made it as a fourth-generation accountant,
with affection and respect.

PREFACE

Writing *The Elusive Art of Accounting* was sort of a de-briefing exercise after thirty years in public practice, a good deal of institute committee work, and some attempt at teaching. It set out the doubts, misgivings, and fitful insights which I had accumulated during my professional career. In the ensuing discussion, I feel that the problems which have worried me have been sorted out into reasonable perspective.

As I see it now, our adherence to cost-based accounting in circumstances in which it is quite inappropriate is so fundamentally misguided that other things that we are doing wrong are scarcely worth worrying about. Cost should not be abandoned as a basis of accounting, but our devotion to it must be modified as a necessary first step to any further progress. It is as though, in our accounting development, we had proceeded up a blind alley, and now find ourselves facing a blank wall. This is not a revolutionary, offbeat view, but a view widely and soberly held by leaders of the accounting profession. For instance, the current president of The American Institute of Certified Public Accountants has expressed the matter in this way:

> Our present efforts to communicate financial data to users are grossly ineffective. I do not know what can be done about it. I am not sure whether we are at fault or the public is at fault. But I have a strong feeling that our statements are as unintelligible to the public as would be the case if they were written in a foreign language. A new look is in order. Perhaps the accounting profession should call on specialists in other fields —behavioral scientists, marketing experts, commercial artists—to help design the new look. Somehow we must find a better way to communicate the meaning of accounting data to nonaccountants. A creative study of the problem might devise a completely new communication medium.*

No amount of ingenious rationalizing or elaboration of definitions can conceal the fact that we must accept this challenge and set about developing a proper system of financial reporting based on values that are currently relevant.

The deeply entrenched opposition to this innocent and basically self-evident proposal is based on two points. Firstly, it is sometimes argued that our economy will run satisfactorily with decision-makers basing

*Marvin L. Stone, in *Empirical Research in Accounting: Selected Studies*, 1968.

themselves on cost data that includes completely obsolete figures. Secondly, there is the fear that attempts at current valuation, because they depart from the solid ground of cost, cannot be relied upon. These two criticisms are of very different weight. The first criticism—that decision-makers do not want to know current values even if they are available—is so patently silly that those who urge it must surely do so on the grounds of the second objection mentioned above; namely, that cost is the only sufficiently reliable base for accounting data. Thus, opposition to current values must boil down to the question of how reliable they can be.

This is a real question and not one to be dogmatically answered. I have no hope that the feasibility of current values can be established by pronouncements of individuals, committees, or institutes. The question will only be answered in the arena of actual financial-statement production. I have never advocated the complete abandoning of cost in the preparation of statements, since I believe it has wide relevance; but unless we accept quite drastic modification of our cost base, I despair of our ever obtaining better statements.

In accounting research at this moment, what we need is to throw a key block—to commit ourselves to the desirability of current values. This would free those who are responsible for publishing statements to push ahead with experiments which would ultimately establish how far the cost basis can be modified by appraisals, price indices, and other devices aimed at up-to-date valuation. The purpose of this book, then, is to throw this key block—to set out the case for current values and to explain how those who publish statements should set about introducing them.

May I once again be forgiven for avoiding the invidious and, indeed, impossible task of referring specifically to the very many colleagues, friends, and enemies who have contributed to the development of the ideas that are expressed in this book. There have been so many who have helped—in particular, perhaps, the enemies.

Howard Ross

Montreal, 1969

Table of Contents

*In view of the opening door to greater participation by account-
ants in basic investment planning, it is particularly desirable that
the profession broaden its outlook and move away from those
policies and procedures which are supported by convention but
are not grounded in economic reality.*

From Paton, *On Accounting*

*So let us get on with the job and do something about the chang-
ing prices problem on the basis of current market buying prices,
instead of delaying action while arguing about theoretical differences which might not amount to much practical significance
anyway. It is certain that accounting systems so based will produce answers much closer to the truth than if we continue with
historical costs.*

From a speech by Reg. S. Gynther, Professor of Accountancy
at the University of Queensland

It is better to be vaguely right than precisely wrong.

A comment attributed to John Meynard Keynes, which, whether he
said it or not, should be seized upon as a guiding principle by anyone who wants to produce a better financial statement.

CHAPTER 1

The Advent of Paper Work

If we are to get better accounting, we must be quite clear about what accounting is. Accounting is the handmaid of business and government, and of many other agencies of endeavour.

Businesses range from the extremely simple to the very complex. Let us start with the simple case of the vendor of roasted chestnuts with his sidewalk brazier. While his operations don't look terribly complicated, he has, in fact, to keep making decisions—the outcome of which will determine whether or not he is a successful chestnut vendor. He must keep an eye on his supply of chestnuts and charcoal, and he watches the condition of his stock. Are the chestnuts drying out to the point that they must be used quickly? Are they in good condition, or have the mice got at some of them? Is it a good growing season, with promise of plentiful and cheap supplies in the future? He must also watch the weather; and if it starts to rain, he must take appropriate precautions. He observes his customers. Are they happy about the extra two cents he is now charging? Do they like the little paper bags he is using in place of the conventional newspaper spills? There are many problems in even this simple kind of venture, and no doubt some chestnut vendors turn out to be unable to cope with them—and so go out of business. However, all of these problems, and the decisions which must be made in handling them, have this in common—they are all under the direct observation of the decision-maker.

Each of the chestnut vendor's basic problems is also present in the operation of a large modern corporation. But the increase in size introduces some entirely new factors. Perhaps the most obvious of these is

1

the fact that decisions must be made by a very large number of people; and of course it follows that a system of communication must be developed to enable all the decisions to be co-ordinated into an intelligent management policy. Here, we immediately get into the mass of paperwork and electronic recording that constitutes the accounting system. The need of communication among those who run the business introduces all sorts of new problems. But we must take particular notice of one fundamental change. The decision-maker is no longer in actual touch with the facts of the venture which he is helping to manage. Normally, the purchasing agent will never see the goods he is purchasing. On his instructions, they may be delivered to a warehouse a thousand miles away—a warehouse, in fact, that he has never even visited. He must act, not on his observation of the goods in inventory, but on what the accounting system reports the situation to be. Similarly, the sales manager will never meet most of those who buy the company's product; nor is the treasurer likely to know any of the bondholders.

It seems to me that there emerges here the most basic fact regarding the accounting system. The system must mirror, as faithfully as it can manage to do so by means of figures, the economic facts which it reports. All decision-makers want to know accurately what is going on, and as they cannot observe the actual occurrences, their next best choice is to obtain clear reports on them. This must seem a rather fatuous truism, and probably no one would attempt to deny it in so many words. But as we shall see later, it is not a proposition on which accountants consistently base themselves when determining their principles or rules of reporting.

For some purposes, it is satisfactory for accounting reports to be stated in terms other than monetary units: for example, quantities of goods, machine or man hours, number of revolutions, and so on. However, if it is to be done as promptly, reliably, and economically as possible, this sort of direct accounting will create problems of control, processing, and analysing. But the major problems in accounting do not arise here. Such problems arise only when we face the necessity of converting the non-monetary elements in the equation to monetary equivalents. Let us pause briefly to be sure of the implications of this crucial point.

It would be difficult to think of a word that is used with more different meanings than the word "value." To an accountant, value is simply the appropriate cash equivalent for any asset involved in the accounting process. It is the common denominator to which all economic facts must be converted in order to produce some necessary reports.

To return to our chestnut vendor. Many of his observations are non-monetary—the size of the passing crowd which constitutes his clientele, the approaching thunderstorm that will interrupt his business, and so on. He must somehow synthesize as many of these data as possible in making such decisions as whether or not to put on more charcoal or whether or not to buy a larger brazier. He works out a course of action; and the more intelligent he is, the more of these factors he will take into consideration and the better he will assess the weight to give to each of them—in other words, the more profitably he will run his business.

In the operation of a large corporation, there must be some decision-making process which is analogous to the synthesis that the chestnut vendor carries out in his head. And since a large corporation will deal with a great mass of reported figures, there must be some recognized and agreed-upon way of producing overall integrated data in an intelligible form. There are many different types of situation to contend with here. For example, the decision to commit an idle plant to a certain type of production is quite different from the decision to build a new plant to produce the product. In the former instance, the productive capacity already exists. The decision may be that it is less costly to let the machine stand idle than it is to put it into production; but as certain costs are involved in shut-down machines, it may well prove advantageous to undertake production. Whereas if a new plant had to be acquired, a quite different calculation would be needed. In the first instance, we would have a situation which involves what accountants call "incremental costs," but such costs would have no relevance in deciding whether or not to build a new plant. Thus, accountants have had to develop various methods of presenting financial data which are to be used in different situations. Probably the most important of these (and certainly from a technical standpoint the most interesting) are the kind of statements that have been devised to give a general overview of the financial strength and profitability of an enterprise. It is here that we encounter the "generally accepted accounting principles" about which we hear so much.

The justification for attempting such a difficult task as presenting a generalized view of large and complex corporations is that, while different types of statements are needed for different purposes, some summarized general picture, brought up to date at regular intervals, is absolutely essential to many of the people who are interested in the business. The contribution of the accounting profession to solving this difficult problem has been the development of the familiar balance sheet and income statement.

Ideally, the overall view should take into consideration all the factors that bear, in any way, on the prosperity of the enterprise (either favourably or unfavourably) and should convert these to their cash equivalent. In this way, an aggregate of favourable factors can be calculated in one dollar total. By deducting the aggregate of the un-favourable factors, we would then end up with the value of the enter-prise stated in dollars. The difference in this figure from period to period would indicate the profit or loss during the interval. This profit or loss might equally well be calculated by valuing the favourable and un-favourable developments which affect the enterprise during the interval, and by striking a balance between them. Happily, through the invention of double-entry bookkeeping, both of these calculations are carried out simultaneously, and we can check profit as reported in the income account with the increase in value that is indicated by the new balance sheet.

The complexity of the accounting art with which this book is con-cerned arises from the difficulty of producing a simplified overview of an extremely complex kind of operation. To find out what is wrong with our accounting system (and also to appreciate what is right) will involve a patient analysis of the problem in depth. At the outset, it is important to recognize that our whole object is to provide decision-makers (who have no opportunity of contact with economic realities) with reports which give them as clear a picture as possible of what is going on.

CHAPTER 2

Present Discontents

Accountants have never had it so good. Today, no other profession is growing so fast. The big problem facing practitioners now is how to handle the work that pours in on them. How can they recruit and train enough good staff to keep up with the natural growth of their practices? This is not an easy atmosphere in which to develop self-criticism. Nevertheless, there are problems with which we should be concerned.

We have, indeed, the best system of financial communication anyone has ever had. For one thing, other civilizations never had the electronic computer. In fact, they did not even have the ballpoint pen. The financial statements and reporting systems that are commonplace today are incomparably better than were those of the philosophic Greeks, the litigious Romans, the scholarly men of the Renaissance, or the mysterious Chinese. Looking back at even shorter range, the statements published today are more informative and more reliable than were those issued a generation ago. By every sort of comparison, we are doing well—except by the one really vital comparison—namely, the comparison between what we are producing and what is needed. We could not be probing outer space with rockets if it were not for electronic data processing, and this is only the most dramatic illustration of our need for reporting and controls in a society in which the handling of complex problems has become routine work.

Solid accounting textbooks; respectable, well-filled professional journals; the sober, weighty releases of our accounting institutes—all these reflect the attention and concern which are now being given the subject of financial reporting. The accounting profession regards itself (quite properly, I think) as the official custodian of the art of financial reporting. This being the case, the profession should feel committed to a continuing appraisal of the art—but an appraisal made in a judicious spirit, pitched somewhere between the mood of self-congratulation of the after-dinner speeches at gatherings of accountants and the mood of abysmal self-abasement of the General Confession in the Book of Common Prayer.

There is certainly some criticism being made. But is there enough? I believe that criticisms of financial statements tend, most of the time, to run along well below crisis level. When a scandal breaks, there are anguished outcries. Investment analysts and relatively well-informed observers (like the financial page editors), all of whom normally take an indulgent, avuncular view of financial statements, turn suddenly to shrill protest and recrimination. The government security regulatory agencies come out with warlike pronouncements. But the scandal eventually fades, and everyone settles down to low-level grumbling. If the scandal gets enough attention, some new pronouncement may come out (from regulatory agencies or professional institutes) which sharpens a definition here or tightens a regulation there, but which does not produce any improvement that I would describe as basic. The general line of criticism, in a soft key, and normally somewhat sharpened when a financial scandal gets into the headlines, is based on three points:

1) *Complaint of lack of comparability in the statements of similar corporations*

All respectable companies (and some that are not respectable) produce statements that are prepared on what are described as "generally accepted accounting principles." This sounds all right. But because these principles authorize several different treatments of important transactions, it follows that two companies may report their financial results in accordance with accepted principles—and yet compile their figures quite differently. This is regrettable, since comparisons between the statements of different companies are such a basic part of financial analysis that a lack of comparability is extremely serious.

The cure would seem to be simple: just agree on a set of accounting principles which does not countenance different treatments of identical transactions. It must be admitted that the accounting profession has been in deadly earnest in tackling this problem. But its attempts have been marked by a persistent lack of achievement which makes the pursuit of the Holy Grail in chivalric times seem like the instant success story of the TV commercials.

2) *Failure to disclose essential information*

It can be argued that even if different principles are applied in similar circumstances, no serious reader will be misled so long as there is adequate disclosure. Government regulatory agencies have tended to be almost obsessed by this point. It is by no means a complete cure, but it is nevertheless a good thing to keep plugging. In any event, thanks to the long campaign in favour of greater disclosure, this is probably less a problem than it was previously.

3) *Failure to show the "real" position*

There is an uneasy feeling that the profit and loss account does not show "real" income, and that the balance sheet docs not show "real" values. Here, we become involved in questions of semantics. Strictly speaking, there is no such thing as "real" or "true" profits, but merely profits which are appropriately calculated for this or that purpose. What is really complained of is that the financial statements produced by accountants do not, in certain important respects, reflect economic facts. This is sometimes explained by claiming that the economist's concept of income is different from the accountant's; but any notion that there are two useful and legitimate ways of looking at the operations of an enterprise simply will not do. The economist and the accountant do have different points of view in financial reporting, because the economist *uses* the statements and the accountant *prepares* them. But it does not follow from this that there should be two types of statement. What does follow is that financial statements must always be a practical compromise between what the user (that is, the economist) would like to have and what the accountant feels he can reliably produce. In this context, the economist should be thought of as the typical statement-user, because, while there is a great variety of statement-users (each of whom may have a distinctive view of his own), the majority of statement-users are nevertheless basically interested in economic factors.

The Accounting Process: A Basic Review

The ineffably simple burden of all three of these criticisms is that financial statements do not tell those who use them what they need to know. What is wrong is not insufficiently-refined concepts, but a basically false starting point—a flaw which is so obvious that it not only escapes attention, but is often not recognized when pointed out. Let us get right back to fundamentals.

Those who study the financial statements of an enterprise want to know (for any one of a variety of reasons) what its financial strength is. This may be because they want to buy it or sell it, to lend it money or borrow from it, to tax it fairly, to estimate its competitive position, to calculate its contribution to the national economy—or for any one of a dozen other reasons. In every case, it is the enterprise's financial strength that must be weighed—not its moral qualities, or its sociability, or its beauty, but its financial stature.

The wealth of any commercial enterprise must be judged from two points of view—and this is true both of large public corporations and of small private corporations, and indeed is true also of partnerships or sole traders. In the first place, the enterprise has a certain amount of wealth; and, in the second place, it has an ability to produce more wealth. Most people dealing with the enterprise want information on both these subjects—how much has the enterprise now, and how much is it likely to have in the future? This point has been put clearly and concisely thus: "Conceptually, the economic position of a company is a composite of the net resources over which the company has control and the prospects for increases or decreases in these net resources."[1]

Balance Sheet and Income Statement

The conventional balance sheet and income statement are supposed to supply the basic information under each of these headings, the balance sheet showing the present wealth of the enterprise and the income statement indicating its earning power. All this seems admirable enough; but there is a serious catch. Largely for historical reasons (and as explained elsewhere in this text), accountants have produced their balance sheets on a basis of cost, rather than on a basis of value. And when this is pointed out, instead of recognizing that a way is being opened up for the production of much more useful statements, they persist in trying to defend that which is clearly indefensible.

It is, of course, a gross oversimplification to suggest that the accountant chooses cost instead of value. The relation between cost and value in accounting is, in fact, subtle and complex. (This relationship

1. John K. Simmons, "A Concept of Comparability in Financial Reporting," *The Accounting Review*, October 1967, p. 681.

will be further explored in the next chapter.) But it is nevertheless true that our present conventional statements are essentially cost-based. And no amount of accounting research, round-table discussion, or fine argument will produce much better statements until we turn our backs resolutely on the double talk and sophistry by which the cost basis, or modified cost basis, is defended.

As a matter of fact, accountants do talk in terms of value (when it suits them) and in certain moods would protest that this was their basic concern. But they do not pursue value consistently. When I wrote *The Elusive Art of Accounting*, I searched out two sharply conflicting pronouncements made by the AICPA. These statements read as follows: "A balance sheet is a statement of the financial condition of the enterprise"; and "A balance sheet does not purport to reflect and could not usefully reflect the value of the enterprise."

It took some looking to find this delightfully parallel wording, but the conflicting claims are common in accounting literature. Accountants argue that they are dealing in values (as indeed they must) when they are trying to describe the purpose of their professional exertions. It would take some pretty sophisticated talk for someone who is preparing a balance sheet to explain his activities in any other terms. What else could he claim to be doing except establishing the current value of the enterprise? On the other hand, when it is pointed out to the accountant that some of his most cherished procedures do not seem even to be aimed at reaching a current value, he replies that they are not intended to.

As suggested above, there are two essential questions relating to an enterprise's wealth: (1) how much has it got, and (2) how much has it the power to produce? The balance sheet is supposed to answer the first of these questions—and goodness knows, current values, and not costs, are what are wanted in that statement. On the other hand, the income statement is supposed to provide a basis on which anyone can inform himself about the enterprise's ability to product wealth—that is to say, its earning power. Here, the cost-value comparison is a little more indirect.

There arc all sorts of ways of investigating earning power. But, as talk is cheap and sales pitches can be devastating, there is much to be said for the practice of judging future prospects on the solid facts of past performance. The accountant's objective here is to set down what has happened in the past in a manner which makes it useful in projecting future probabilities. Here, there is, *prima facie*, no obvious reason to prefer value over cost, and the matter must be considered more deeply.

Let us first take the case of an individual. In trying to establish how productive he is likely to be, it is often sufficient to find what his current rate of salary is. In fact, in hiring an individual (which is where this kind of question is likely to arise), his current rate of remuneration will usually be the fact most seriously considered. When the situation is not so simple (for example, where the individual has been running a business), the most likely approach in judging his earning power may be to examine a financial statement for his business. If the business is in the nature of a venture, the statement might be for the most recent venture managed by the individual. This venture might have covered a few weeks or even a period of several years. In either case, a set of statements based on cost might be perfectly satisfactory—for, as explained later, cost is the appropriate basis for venture accounting.

However, if we are dealing not with an individual but with a complex modern public corporation, venture accounting (and the cost basis) is wholly inappropriate. The corporation may well be engaged in all sorts of ventures. But at any given point in time, these will be at various stages of completion, and it will therefore be quite impossible to establish the corporation's earning power by a venture-type financial statement. It is for this reason that the annual-income concept was developed. An income statement purports to show (and should show more unequivocally than do conventional statements) the earnings of the corporation over the past year. As will be argued exhaustively later, this cannot be done satisfactorily other than by statements which are unflinchingly based on current values.

A Matter of Principle or of Utility?

A point of capital significance emerges from this discussion. Accounting is not based on "fundamental principles" in any recognized sense of these words, but on sheer utility or usefulness. A balance sheet must be made up on the basis of current values if it is to make sense to anyone studying the financial stature of an enterprise. But a balance sheet that is prepared on the conventional modified cost basis now in use may be satisfactory for some purposes—for example, in establishing for a banker that he can safely extend a line of credit. Similarly, an income statement may be satisfactory on a cost basis for some purposes—for example, where venture accounting is appropriate. But for the annual statements of a large commercial corporation, current values alone make sense.

Thus, even such a fundamental question as whether to use cost or value as the basis for our statements is not a matter of principle, but simply a question of which provides the more useful information in any given case. It is not the thesis of this book that current-value accounting is intrinsically superior to any other kind—it is simply that current-value accounting is most appropriate for the annual published financial statements of large corporations. Throughout this text, it is the published reports of commercial corporations with which we shall be concerned. These reports present special problems of their own. (Some comments on the accounting problems of other types of enterprise are contained in Chapter 7.)

We may sum up, at this point, by saying that the crucial defect in published statements is that they are based on cost rather than on value —a blunt assertion which will be examined more fully in the next chapter. Two consequences follow from this: (1) statement-users do not get as satisfactory data as they might be provided with; and (2) all attempts to improve financial reporting are frustrated from the start.

CHAPTER 3

Cost and Value

Let us now look more closely at this question of cost and value that is so fundamental to an understanding of financial reporting. Professor Paton puts the matter with absolute clarity when he says that cost is important to the accountant when it indicates value—and not otherwise. He is supported by the authors of *AICPA Research Study No. 3*, who quote him with approval. This concept of the relationship between cost and value retains an enormous importance for the role of cost in the preparation of statements. Even if *current value* is accepted as our proper goal, such current value will normally be established by reference to *cost*. The cost of an article, if recent, and in the absence of peculiar circumstances, will normally be as good an indication of value as we can get or could want. In the vast majority of accounting circumstances, cost and value are therefore identical. The whole argument arises where cost, for one reason or another, ceases to be a good indication of value. This may affect a relatively small percentage of the items handled—but these items may have a decisive effect on the reliability of the resulting statements.

I have described our present statements as "cost based," but have hastened to add that this is an oversimplification. While we have been led to rely too much on cost, we have not been unaware that cost must be modified for some purposes. In fact, a strict 100 percent reliance on cost could produce patently absurd results. Where accountants have gone wrong is not in failing to see that cost must be modified in order to avoid absurdities, but in the way in which they have gone about modifying it.

If an attempt were made to draw up rules for the preparation of balance sheets and income statements without any reference to how these statements had evolved in the past, almost inevitably a thorough-going value base would be selected. It is common for accounting teachers, when they are introducing a new class of students to the balance sheet, to observe that the statement is immediately understood. It is easy for beginners to appreciate that assets are the valuable things owned and that liabilities are the amounts owed—with the simple corollary that the difference between the two represents the wealth of the enterprise. This is exactly what any sensible person would have expected. The trouble comes when, having introduced this simple equation, the teacher must then proceed to explain that the amounts shown for assets are, in many cases, not what the assets are worth, but are amounts which result from the application of something called "generally accepted accounting principles" to certain past transactions. And when the student later goes on to discover that the leaders of the profession are still arguing among themselves as to which principles really are generally accepted (and, indeed, whether they are properly described as "principles" at all), it is easy to appreciate the basically unsatisfactory situation into which we have gotten ourselves.

It would, of course, be much more satisfactory if the accounting class could continue to assume that figures on the asset side did constitute an attempt to set down the value of things owned, and that the stated liabilities did constitute an effort to measure indebtedness—with the net of the two thus establishing the wealth of the enterprise at the balance-sheet date. It would surely not be difficult to move from this point to a discussion of the difficulties encountered in providing a realistic meaurement of some kinds of assets and liabilities. And by doing so, we would have then established the tentative nature of even the best of financial statements. But unfortunately, accounting statements did not evolve in so straightforward a manner. Accounting statements have been developed, over very long periods of time, by practical accountants who met each problem as it arose and thus kept establishing precedents which were gradually built into the accounting process. Thus, it is natural that after years of recording income and outgo, accountants should be strongly oriented towards transactions. And when the need for a balance sheet first became apparent, it was also natural for them to develop one on a cost basis—since cost is essentially a transaction-type concept.

However, as I have pointed out earlier, a balance sheet that is based strictly on cost would often be absurd. For example, no one would think of recording goods on hand at cost if they had obviously deteriorated in condition since the time that they were purchased. It seemed a sensible step, then, to write down the cost of such goods in such a way as to reflect the deterioration or loss of value; and from this practice was gradually developed the highly cherished rule of "anticipate all probable losses." This was going far enough in the early days of accounting, because statements were needed largely for credit purposes and the important thing was to deal in figures which at least did not overstate values. Understatements were not objectionable, and in fact were thought praiseworthy in the interests of what accountants described as "conservatism"—a term implying great reliability.

Thus, the apparently safe rule of anticipating losses became deeply imbedded in accounting thinking, without any accompanying rule to cover anticipated profits. This was a clear-cut triumph of prudence over logic, and it had a profound and lasting effect on accounting. As time passed, other valuation problems were met in the same way, and financial reporting became riddled with downward adjustments of cost—while write-ups, in opposite situations (that is, when value had increased), were regarded as highly reprehensible.

While it is easy to understand how this came about, this does not mean that it makes sense. No one knows better than accountants that every commercial transaction has two sides. Accountants invented double-entry bookkeeping; and when, at the Ninth International Congress of Accountants (in Paris in 1967), the president quoted the great German philosopher, Goethe, as saying that "double-entry bookkeeping is one of the most beautiful inventions of the human mind," probably no accountant present found the statement extravagant or excessively laudatory. And yet, bearing in mind that the very essence of double-entry bookkeeping is that every transaction can be viewed from two sides, how strange it is that accountants have come, in developing their modifications of cost, to think of only one side—to protect scrupulously the purchaser, the lender, or the taxpayer, and to exhibit a callous disregard for the interests of the vendor, the borrower, and the tax collector.

In some of his activities, the accountant is avowedly (and quite properly) representing his employer or his client. When he is acting for, say, a prospective purchaser, he is entitled to (and must) use his skill to protect the interests of that purchaser. However, when the accountant is preparing financial statements which are to be published by a public corporation, he is in a quasi-judicial position. The statements he issues, while usually prepared officially for the shareholders of the corporation, are also intended to circulate more generally and to guide those who deal with the corporation in many different situations—hence the description, "general purpose statements." It is thus imperative that such statements should not just present a "safe" picture which shows somewhat less than the value of the concern; the statements must show, as fairly as it can be shown, what the value of the corporation actually is—and this both from a net-asset and an earning-power point of view.

There are tremendous difficulties in producing such a picture (including some problems which are virtually insoluble), but if this is not at least our goal, we can never expect to produce the best statements of which we are capable.

(Incidentally, the auditor, in respect to accounting principles, is in precisely the same position as the accountant. He too is in a quasi-judicial position. The financial reports to the shareholders are accompanied by his professional opinion, which states (in one way or another) that the shareholders, for whom they are prepared, may rely on the statements. He should have just as much in mind the interests of the shareholder who wishes to sell shares as the shareholder who wishes to buy more.)

To put the matter succinctly, the basic difference between what we *are* doing and what we *should* be doing is just this:

1) *Present convention*

We rely on cost where this does not seem excessive. We write down cost when we feel that value may have dropped. We refuse to write up values above cost, even when they have clearly risen.

2) *Proper objective*

We should start with the assumption (surely not a preposterous one) that we are to produce statements which give the best approximation of values that we can achieve. In most instances, cost will no doubt provide the valuation we are looking for. We will accept the conventional write-downs of cost where these seem appropriate. In fact, the only departure from current practice is that we will recognize write-ups where these are appropriate. This we will do on the assumption that it is no more dangerous to adjust in one direction than in the other—and no less essential either, since for every purchaser there is a vendor, and for every lender a borrower.

It would be easy to find statements by high accounting authorities to the effect that an understatement of asset values is just as obnoxious as an overstatement. In fact, we all keep saying this. The trouble is that when we get down to the actual process of statement preparation, we do not act as though we believed it.

It is odd that this point still has to be argued. It is not only self-evident, but has been insisted upon time and again in accounting writing —but without anyone paying much attention to it. To take only one example from among the many that might be selected; in a recent issue of *The Accounting Review* we read:

> . . . we accept a subjective estimate of useful life because we must in order to have a figure for depreciation. And we want that depreciation figure because we believe it is useful. So accountants do sometimes sacrifice objectivity for the sake of utility; but they do so selectively and according to no general rule.[2]

To appreciate fully the illogic of currently accepted practice, it is necessary to remember one further source of confusion. The writing-down of cost when values drop is only required in the case of some types of asset —namely, those classified as "current assets." There are other types of assets where write-downs are not insisted upon when values fall, and where write-ups in value may be sanctioned in some circumstances.

Objective for Accountants

We started out by saying that the essential reform in accounting consisted of moving from cost-based statements to value-based statements. We have perhaps advanced the discussion far enough at this point to restate this basic proposition somewhat more precisely.

The proposal is that we move from an accounting which is primarily based on cost, with mandatory downward revision of current assets when values fall and a conglomeration of special rules (many of them optional) for write-downs and write-ups of non-current assets, to an accounting based on a consistent attempt at establishing current values for all assets—with the recognition that in many instances (perhaps in most instances) cost may be our best indication of actual value. Under the new accounting, cost would be very important; but it would not be our primary objective. Our primary objective would be current-

2. J. M. Fremgen, "Utility and Accounting Principles," *The Accounting Review*, July 1967, p. 461.

value statements, using cost where it gives us the best approach to such values.

Accounting Principles (Ground Rules)

Here emerges the reason for all the troubles that we have had in agreeing on a statement of accounting principles which are generally accepted. It is often said that an authoritative group should get together and produce a statement of generally accepted accounting principles. The implication is that this is a new idea and that no authoritative group has ever made a serious attempt to produce such a statement. But this is simply not true. Every accounting textbook represents an effort to set forth accounting principles that are generally accepted. Indeed, some texts do this at great length. However, none of these attempts are entirely satisfactory—because, as our "principles" are illogical, we inevitably end up with a statement which is neither logical, consistent, nor satisfactory. With adjustments to cost in one direction only (i.e., downward), no "principles" can be made to appear logical. Moreover, as the adjustments are essentially arbitrary, there must inevitably be several equally defensible ways of making them—and we encounter here the sanction of alternative treatments which destroy the comparability that is so important to analysts.

We will return to this subject in Chapter 6 and there argue that the acceptance of current values as the primary basis of accounting would provide a logical basis for our principles. This would in turn make the production of a code of principles possible, and perhaps not even very difficult.

Two Conundrums

The case for current values is so completely unanswerable (even when put forward in the moderate and guarded terms which I have been careful to use) that we must ask two questions:

(1) Why have accountants so consistently refused to heed the many distinguished advocates of a better system?

and (2) Why do those who use statements not only fail to mount any sustained clamour of complaint, but seem bent on discouraging any attempt at introducing more useful forms of presentation?

These are good questions. They puzzled me for a while, but I think now that I understand the reasons for the undoubted general acquiescence in the present type of product. Let me try to explain.

The View of Accountants

I find the accountants' complacency relatively easy to understand. The accountant is basically interested in statement production. To produce financial statements promptly for the large modern corporation is a fiendishly difficult task at best. The accountant who has the awesome responsibility for issuing the statement (being human, despite some opinions to the contrary) must inevitably think of the tremendous risks that he is taking—as well as of the requirements of those for whose use the statements are intended. No wonder accountants are labelled "conservative"—meaning that they prefer the devil they know to the devil they don't know.

Moreover, modern statements have developed over a couple of hundred years—from the simple recording of receipts and disbursements, to joint venture accounting, through simple balance sheets for credit purposes, right up to the modern concern for accurate income determination. As time went on and things became more complicated, more sophisticated financial statements eventually became necessary. Accountants tended to attempt to produce these by improving and tinkering with the cost-based statements with which they had started out, instead of launching out boldly into some more suitable type of statement. With great ingenuity, accountants have continued to produce more-or-less workable statements by improving disclosure and by refining certain areas (such as inventory valuation) where troubles developed.

In short, accountants have been almost totally absorbed in coping with the day-to-day problems brought on by the onward creeping of new complexities, and have therefore been willing to settle for a policy which Damon Runyan would have described as "doing the best they can." They have made cautious adjustments to existing practice as new problems arose, and they have generally turned an unresponsive ear to their colleagues who, from the relative security of academic life, have urged them on to more heroic measures. It is all rather like that poignant scene in Macaulay's *Lays of Ancient Rome*, when the vast Tuscan army surged against Horatius and his two dauntless companions on the bridge, the subsequent confusion being described thus:

> But those behind cried "Forward!"
> And those before cried "Back!"

The Complacent User

It is understandable, I suppose, that the accountant should be inclined to let well enough alone—"well enough" being a state of affairs in which his services are so much in demand that he can claim to belong to the fastest growing profession in the country, and without much fear of rebuttal. I used to think that if only statement-users were consulted, there would be a full-throated chorus of complaint. The extraordinary (and to me disappointing) conclusion to which I have now come is that there is no such pent-up dissatisfaction.

To start with, surprisingly little serious research has been done on the subject of how a statement-user actually goes about using a statement. Social scientists are beginning to take an interest in this question and to consider seriously the mental processes of, say, an investor who is deciding whether to buy or sell a security. We may wait, with what patience we may, for the results of their studies—which may well demonstrate that the investor buys stocks indiscriminately (like the compulsive shopper in the supermarket), or from deep, unresolved psychological tensions (like the man who invests in Colt Industries because of a frustrated wish to own a pony, or in the Armour Company through a secret craving for protection). It will presumably be some time, however, before definitive information is available on this subject; and it is necessary, in the meantime, to venture a few cautious working assumptions. For example, we might start with a recent comment which illustrates what must be a generally accepted hypothesis:

> Managements of large firms probably do not rely on these accounting measures as much as they once did because of their increased awareness of the inherent limitations and biases of these measures for decision-making purposes and their access to better information. Nevertheless, the present and prospective stockholders of large firms, especially those who play little or no role in management policy making, still tend to rely heavily on these accounting measures in deciding whether to buy, sell, or hold shares in these firms. The apparent reason is that these "outside" investors have little access to "hard" information about the firm's present and future prospects other than these measures.[3]

We must remember that a general purpose statement can only provide a limited amount of information and therefore constitutes only a starting point for investigation. For the moment then, let us make the tentative

3. Melvin N. Greenball, "Evaluation of the Usefulness to Investors of Different Accounting Estimations of Earnings," in *Empirical Research in Accounting: Selected Studies*, 1968.

assumption (suggested in Chapter 2) that statements are used to help establish the present strength of a company and its earning power.

Starting, then, with this bold premise, perhaps we are ready to take the next step by agreeing that anyone who uses a statement would prefer to have the assets of the corporation stated at some relevant value. This is so obvious that it seems a pity to spend time making the point; but to hammer the lesson home thus ponderously seems the only way to guard against the apologist who maintains (not consistently, but when it suits him to do so) that a balance sheet does not even purport to show the value of the enterprise.

If statement-users generally want to know the financial strength of an enterprise and are given a set of statements which do not even purport to reflect this, you would naturally expect them to object. But, by and large, they don't. In fact, I have never met a financial analyst who was the least bit interested in a radically new type of statement. Ask him if he is satisfied, and he naturally says that he is not. But ask him what improvements he would suggest, and what does he say? "More information about long-term contracts; greater detail on depreciation policy"— sensible enough, but just a bit pathetic in the light of the basic inadequacies.

It is difficult not to agree with Donald A. Corbin when he says, in *The Accounting Review* of October 1967, that the investment analyst's objection to current values "appears to be the outgrowth of questionable generalization from limited research." Or again: "A previous investigation of their methods at the Forum on Finance [sponsored by New York University] led me to the conclusion that many primarily 'analysed' each other's reports or reported the views of the company managements they were supposed to be analysing."

Undoubtedly, part of the complacency of the financial critics can be attributed to certain deeply-rooted misconceptions. They have allowed themselves to be persuaded that there is great merit in what is described as "conservatism"—which is simply the conviction that no mis-statement matters so long as it is on the low side for assets or income, or on the high side for liabilities and expenses. Moreover, they have also come to believe that there are compensating values in our present type of statement—values, for example, like objectivity. Objectivity implies a decision on the valuation of an asset which is not based on the opinion of someone who has a personal interest in the matter. It is undoubtedly a highly desirable quality in financial reporting, but quite often it is as attainable in current valuation as it is in cost. To take the simplest possible case: if a corporation holds an investment in marketable securities, the current market price is just as objective a figure as the original cost to the corporation.

However, all this is peripheral. There are really two important reasons why the present type of statement has such a devoted following among statement-users. Firstly, there is the simple fact that the present type of statement is really not too bad (I argue only that it could be much better); and secondly, there is the subtle but powerful interest in maintaining the *status quo*. Let us take a look at each of these reasons individually.

Present Merits

I think it extraordinary that the most prevalent complaint about our financial statements attacks them at what I consider their strongest point —that is, on the consistency of their principles and procedures. In spite of the fact that alternative procedures are sanctioned at various points in the preparation of financial statements, our present accounting system is based on a fairly well-organized and consistent set of principles and procedures.

While it is true that the investment analyst is presented with a balance sheet in which at least some important assets are stated on a cost basis which may have very little relevance to current valuations, and as some of these costs eventually get charged off to earnings, the unsatisfactory base applies not only to the balance sheet, but also to the income statement. Thus, the all-important figure of net income is calculated on a mixture of current and past values which is theoretically quite indefensible. Nevertheless, the fact remains that the resulting reported income, even if it does not accurately reflect the economic facts of life, is at least prepared under a reasonably explicit set of rules.

Let us put ourselves in the investment analyst's shoes. What he has to do is to decide which shares are likely to rise most quickly or to drop most slowly. He will often consider investing in mortgages, bonds, real estate, and so on, but the really tough questions arise in connection with appraising shares, and we will therefore concentrate on this aspect of the analyst's work. In this area, his whole problem is in the relative market price of the shares of different corporations, and what such relative prices may be expected to be in the future. In making his judgment, he naturally takes into account all sorts of factors. In part, he presumably relies on the conventional balance sheet and income statements which companies issue to their shareholders at regular intervals. From these statements, he knows what dividends a company pays and what dividends it has paid in the past. He also knows what earnings are reported and what earnings have been reported in the past. Since conventional statements (in spite of what everyone says about alternatives and inconsistencies) are based on a relatively well-organized system, the analyst can project with reasonable confidence what future dividends and future reported profits are likely to be—and, in this way, he decides which securities should be bought and which should be sold. As previously mentioned, he naturally takes other factors into consideration; but the projected trends from past performance in dividend payments and reported profits are certainly of basic interest.

It does not worry the analyst that reported profits are not really calculated in a way which reflects economic results as closely as possible—because reported profits are the only financial data an analyst has to go on, and he knows that others are also watching these reported profits. Thus, in the demand-supply equation for any security, what is important is not the so-called *real* profits (which no one has any way of estimating under our present system), but rather the *reported* profits. If the shares of two corporations sell at the same price, and from a projection of past trends the dividends and reported earnings of one are likely to rise faster than those of the other, then it is time to switch from the corporation with the slower-moving trend to the corporation with the better prospects—other things being equal. (It is important to notice here that the analyst is not primarily concerned with whether or not a company is well managed, whether or not it is producing a good product, or even whether or not it is earning profits. His primary interest is in how the price of its shares is likely to move.)

Therefore, while an investment analyst may not know what the real economic results of a corporation have been (and thus cannot project what they will be), nevertheless he can make reasonable decisions on the basis of the only financial information available—in the confidence that other buyers and sellers in the market will be using these same figures. He has, therefore, some kind of an indicator.

The situation is a little like that of a golfer in a tournament who must adhere to a strict set of rules or restrictions in trying to get around the course. It is true that these restrictions hamper him, but because his competitors must also abide by the same set of rules, he is not at a disadvantage when compared with them. And playing the stock market is rather like playing a game. Looked at with strict logic, every time a share is bought and sold, someone is right and someone is wrong. The buyer is backing his judgment against the seller's, and if they are both kept equally in the dark by being given data which is less informative than it might be, there is no reason for either of them to complain.

The Case of the Candid Chairman

Looking at the meticulous figures "in serried ranks assembled" which the investor gets in a set of financial statements, it may be hard to appreciate that he is getting a sort of vague gesture from management to indicate roughly the direction in which the enterprise is heading, and not a serious summary of the economic facts. Yet that is what he is getting. This was never more clearly (or more charmingly) demonstrated than is a classical exchange between Mr. Arthur Chamberlain, chairman of several prominent companies in England at the time, and that fine professional journal, *The Accountant*. This was way back in the mid-1930's; but the dialogue deserves to be preserved.

Mr. Chamberlain, as the chairman of several corporations, used to take the occasion provided by the annual meetings of such corporations to expound his highly sophisticated notions of financial reporting. In 1935, at the annual meeting of Tube Investments, Ltd., he took the occasion to remark (with what *The Accountant* described as "shocking frankness") to his stockholders:

> I do not suppose there are many of my audience who are simple enough to believe that a company's accounts, particularly a holding company, set forth the actual and exact profits earned in each year . . . I do not think it would be too cynical to say that the ordinary shareholder is lucky if he can read from the figures of a balance sheet more than an idea of the general tendency forward or backward, *unless the directors are themselves aware of it and wish him to be* . . . I think it desirable to make a few remarks that will enable the inexpert to read our balance sheet and accounts. I have informed you on several occasions that we do not bring into the Tube Investments balance sheet the whole of the profits our activities have created; we bring in only just as much as we require to pay the dividends we recommend and to place to general reserve, or add to the carry forward, so much as we consider will make a pretty balance sheet . . . I do however make one concession to exactitude. If the real earnings for the year are larger than those of the preceding one, the figure shown in the balance sheet will be larger and if they are smaller the balance sheet figure will also be smaller. The increase or decrease will only be a pointer, it will have no actual relation to the real figure.

The Accountant, in a thoroughly civilized British manner, went to bat for the profession. Objecting to the fact that the press had described this as a "stimulating" speech, it asked:

> Why publish accounts at all? Would it not be better if the shareholders were merely told in a directorial report and speech how lovely everything is in the garden? . . . We sincerely hope financial adversity will never come the way of Tube Investments, Ltd., but we feel entitled to wonder what accounting policy Mr. Chamberlain will follow if and when "the real earnings of the year" turn into a minus figure. Presumably "the balance sheet figure will also be smaller" but how will the directors then "make a pretty balance sheet"? . . . The kind of candour which prompts the Chairman of a public meeting to tell his shareholders that the accounts contain "one concession to exactitude" is, in our view, misplaced candour which could be transferred with advantage to the balance sheet itself.

Some time later, at the annual meeting of Roneo, Ltd., of which he was also chairman, Mr. Chamberlain took the opportunity to continue the dialogue. On this occasion, he stated:

> If any shareholder, thinks that our profit of £59,000 is arrived at by the simple use of the addition table he must be lamentably ignorant of how accounts are made up. Our profits are not the sum of certain easily ascertainable and mathematically exact figures.

After expatiating on the difficulty of valuing the multitude of small items which compose payables, receivables, and inventories, he continued:

> I have said enough to show you that an auditor—however capable and however conscientious—is no more able than the staff or anyone else to fix a definite value, from which there can be no escape, on every item, and I would undertake to present figures for this company—which no man on earth, and certainly no auditor, could say were wrong—and which would show our profits today to be at least £25,000 more than you see them, and I would equally undertake to put forward figures equally unchallengeable showing them to be £14,000 less. It is entirely a question of the view taken of an enormous number of probabilities and possibilities, and all you can honestly say is that the one extreme would be very optimistic and the other very pessimistic.

This time, *The Accountant* was perhaps a little softened by a touching tribute to the auditing profession which came at the close of Mr. Chamberlain's address. In summing up, he said: "Auditors are like beer—all auditors are good, but some are better than others—something you could hardly say of any other class or profession." In any event, *The Accountant* closed the exchange by commenting:

> In some measure [readers] may be shocked by the frankness of the speaker regarding company accounts; in part amused by the lightness with which Mr. Chamberlain deals with his subject, but beneath the levity, they will also, we think, discern a considerable measure of sound business sense. No one will question the latitude it is possible to exercise in the computation of business profits.

A lot has happened since 1935. But if anyone of candour equal to Mr. Chamberlain's should ever again be elected chairman of a corporation, we might once again hear equally shocking frankness. The point that Mr. Chamberlain makes about reported earnings being a direction indicator (rather than a serious attempt to reflect economic reality) seems to me to strike at the central fact of our financial statements. In spite of criticisms, we do have a fairly well thrashed-out set of practical rules governing our direction indicators; and the modern investor and analyst can get by, after a fashion, with them. What seems tragic to me is that there is so little apparent enthusiasm for the relatively modest reforms that would enable us to provide much more accurate and reliable indicators—i.e., indicators that would truly reflect the economic facts of life as nearly as they can be reflected in generalized financial statements.

Vested Interests

Another reason why statement-users remain content with an unsatisfactory type of statement arises from what might be described as vested interests in maintaining the *status quo*—a subject so much in the air that it was touched on twice in one recent issue (October 1967) of *The CPA*. In the first instance, that distinguished observer of the profession, John Carey, remarked: "Some critics suggest that the profession's response to challenge is to rationalize that the *status quo* is beyond improvement." In the second instance, Leonard M. Savoie, Executive Vice-President of AICPA, said: "If there is a common experience running through the problems of raising technical standards of the profession, it is that in the face of an irreversible trend towards tighter accounting standards, there persists in some quarters a reluctance to move ahead from the status quo."

The fact that an analyst is in business at all is, *prima facie*, evidence that he is successful. He has learned to operate with the information available. If he is a reflective person, he is sure to be aware of the shortcomings and limitations of the data with which he is working. This in itself gives him a certain confidence and makes him reluctant to abandon the system he understands, even if an alternative type of accounting has theoretical advantages.

Current-value accounting is a logical method of reporting financial transactions and could be used to provide much better information than is now available. But it would involve appraisals and other new techniques with which the practising analyst is perhaps not too familiar. To ask an analyst to support a campaign to switch to current-value accounting is, therefore, to ask him to abandon a method which he understands —in the hope that more useful and reliable information can be produced by a different system. To put it bluntly, the adoption of a new and unfamiliar system may present itself to a highly experienced leader of the consulting profession as an invitation to start competing with the rawest MBA graduate—and without the benefit of painfully accumulated know-how to offset youthful vigour and all the new tricks picked up at college.

What has been said of the investment analyst is, in general, true for investors, shareholders, creditors, and other categories of statement-users. The successful operators in all these fields now have a system which they at least understand, and with which they have learned to make do. None of them can be expected to be enthusiastic, without a good deal of persuasion, about switching to a different and untried system.

The Labour Analogy

In comparing different types of data, an interesting analogy may be drawn between investment problems and labour negotiations. It might be taken for granted that labour unions are interested, not in *money* wages, but in *real* wages. If wage increases result in price increases, there is little to be gained by raising wages. The unions receive many lectures on the importance of concentrating on real wages, but persist in focusing their attention on money wages. The investment analyst is in somewhat the same position. He should be concerned about economic values, but is in fact much more interested in reported accounting data. For want of better figures, everyone must use such information as is available, and it doesn't really matter too much to the analyst whether reported earnings follow economic earnings closely or not.

In spite of this, it remains true of course that while the competitive position of a practising analyst might not be improved by the availability of better figures (that is, figures closer to economic fact), the overall performance of the economy should be improved. It is very much as though a radically new golf ball were introduced—say, a golf ball capable of being hit twice as far as the present ball. This would not necessarily be welcomed by established pros, and might in fact represent for them only difficult problems of adaptation. Nevertheless, it remains true that the introduction of the new ball would lead to much lower scores.

Management's Point of View

We must now consider management's point of view. Managers must use statements in reaching the decisions which they have to make in running their businesses. They have many different kinds of requirements and have need of special studies to make decisions—studies such as those on plant expansion, pricing, inventory policy, and so on. However, management also need a basic overall statement for the whole business, and in this respect are in much the same position as statement-users such as analysts, investors, and creditors. For their own decision-making, therefore, management should want a statement which explains as clearly as possible what is going on; but, like the analyst, management have learned to live with the type of statement they now get. They too prefer the familiar to the untried.

Management's interest, moreover, is twofold. In addition to wanting a statement for their own guidance, they also need a statement to issue to their shareholders. Such a statement gives the owners of the business a report on management's stewardship. The present conventional statements suit management very well for this purpose, because, while they are based on a reasonably well-organized and logical plan, there is enough leeway in determining balance-sheet values to enable management to report in a satisfactory manner—which means, "in a manner that keeps the shareholders happy."

The task of management in a modern corporation is complex and difficult. To understand the decisions they make requires an intimate knowledge of the facts and a variety of highly developed skills. Nothing is more disruptive to management than pressures from shareholders based on inadequate information, and the way to minimize irresponsible questions by the shareholders is to keep reporting to them better and better results. To report a loss, of course, invites a serious investigation; and in these days of rising incomes, it is almost as bad not to report an increase in profit. In these circumstances, any management would like to be able to report steadily increasing profits. (And incidentally, this does

not strike me as being particularly sinister.) They have learned to accomplish this under present ground rules, which allow a certain room for
manoeuvring, and they tend to be content.

The Real Task Ahead

To adopt the current-value concept would not solve all accounting problems at a stroke. In fact, it might well introduce more problems than we
have now. What it would do is to open the way to better statements. It
would enable accounting bodies to get down to work on our real problem
—which is to devise better and better ways of translating the facts of an
enterprise's life into usable financial data. Some problems of asset valuation and income measurement will never be completely solved. But at
least our efforts will be in the right direction—that is, towards a
sensible goal.

CHAPTER 4

The Concept of "Current Value" Explored

It is now necessary to examine the concept of value more closely. The term "current value" has been selected deliberately because it is a vague and ill-defined term. Other kinds of valuation—for example, replacement value, realizable value, market value, or liquidation value—are important and useful in accounting. But each of these terms has acquired a technical meaning which is too restrictive for our main purpose—that purpose being to establish a general concept, free from specific associations, whereby we can agree on the type of value that is appropriate when attempting to produce informative financial statements. The word "current" is essential, as we need a valuation which has relevance at the statement date. In fact "current," in this connection, is a synonym for "relevant." Having chosen a term that is free from prior technical associations, we must now devote ourselves to considering in detail what our concept should be deemed to imply.

Real and Conventional Values

We are, of course, not trying to establish intrinsic or real value in the sense in which such terms are used in, say, the physical sciences. When immersed in the perplexities and vagaries of the accounting art, it would be reassuring to think that there were such things as basic, unarguable principles which we might some day discover—much as Newton discovered gravity and Einstein discovered relativity. But we are fated to labour in the world of commerce, and the world of commerce has none of the certainty of the world of physics. Ours is a more vague and a perhaps less exalted quest—namely, the search for simple usefulness.

What we require, then, is values that are useful. This means values through which data can be presented in a way that is helpful to anyone who is involved in economic activity. We must not expect to discover values that are based on some kind of natural law. Our values must be developed, not discovered, and we may be sure that they will be conventional values—that is, values which are reached by consensus or general agreement.

The reason we need values at all is that if we are to produce a coherent, manageable, and brief statement of a company's financial strength, then we must aggregate a great many dissimilar types of assets and liabilities. We are faced, therefore, with the old problem of adding together apples and oranges. "Valuation" to an accountant is simply the process of converting various assets to their cash equivalent.

An Improbable Occurrence

It is vital that we appreciate all the implications that may be drawn from the accountant's view of the valuation process. In his eyes, the process is a means of converting assets and liabilities to the common denominator of cash so that they can be aggregated and used in measuring wealth. I find it irresistible to conclude that the first historic attempts at producing balance sheets must have been in kind, rather than in terms of money. In fact, I can just picture the scene:

Scene: The Great Hall of that fine old English castle, Dogsberry Towers. The date is 1491, the year before Columbus sailed to America (so that no one on this side of the Atlantic can claim injury from what is said). As the curtain rises, that good, simple-minded old knight, Rodolph the Uninspired, is discovered behind a large table that is littered with bits of paper and slate and sharp stones (the recording implements of the time), amongst which the old fellow is shuffling about, pausing from time to time to scratch a figure laboriously, with much licking of pointed stones. Finally, he gives up in exasperation and bangs loudly on the table with a tankard.

RODOLPH: What ho, without there! Fetch me another double mead—standing up.

VOICE WITHOUT: Coming Sire.

(I originally composed this drama in Middle English, but later found that one of my partners could not understand it. It then occurred to me that there might be others who would be hindered by similar difficulties, and I therefore rendered the scenario in the modern idiom. I feel that it loses something in translation—but, anything for the sake of clarity.)

[*A villein shuffles in with a tankard.*]

ROD: And where is my steward Marmaduke? Is he not yet arrived?

VILLEIN: I was on the point of showing him in, me Lord.

[*He does so. Enter Marmaduke.*]

ROD: Dear Marmaduke! I am so glad to see you. Something terrible has happened—you see before you a ruined man.

MAR: [*Incredulously.*] A ruined man? But, my Lord, you are one of the wealthiest men in Christendom.

ROD: I was once, but I am sinking fast. I have it all here. [*He fumbles about and finally emerges with a piece of slate.*] Yes, since you made up the last statement of my affairs a few years ago, my wealth has declined. Here, let me see . . . [*Reads*] from 812 to 533.

MAR: From 812 to 533? But what figures are these?

ROD: [*Excitedly.*] Well, they are my own invention. You see, I listed down everything I owned—just as you showed me. But when I was finished, I wanted to see whether I was going ahead or behind. So [*with an expression of delight at his own cunning*], I added all the things up. Last time, I had 812 things; this time, 533. It's as simple as that— bankruptcy in a few more years, at this rate.

MAR: But you can't do that. That's like adding apples and oranges.

ROD: What are oranges?

MAR: They are an anachronism. Skip it. (I had forgotten that Columbus had not yet discovered America.) Let's say it's like adding apples and chestnuts.

ROD: Well, what's wrong with that? Three apples and two chestnuts make . . . Let me see . . . Ah . . . yes . . . Five pieces of fruit. Right?

MAR: [*Great effort at control*] I am a member of the Guild of Stewards, after serving the customary 25-year apprenticeship. May I respectfully suggest that you leave these counting matters to me.

ROD: [*Piteously*] But you had taught me to add . . . and I thought you would be so pleased. [*Sniffles pathetically.*].

MAR: [*Relenting*] Look, my Lord. Would you rather have three horses and one rabbit, or one horse and ten rabbits?

ROD: Naturally, I would rather have three horses and one rabbit.

MAR: Quite right. You see, you would be better off with four animals than with eleven. [*His voice gradually rises to a shout as he loses his control.*] BECAUSE THEY ARE NOT THE SAME KIND OF ANIMAL! [*He regains control with an effort and continues more calmly.*] You see, the reason you had so many things at the time of the first count was that you had just bought 500 homing pigeons.

ROD: They were a passing fancy of my wife's. I can deny her nothing.

MAR: Whereas, they are all gone now.

ROD: [*Indulgently*] She changed her mind, the little dear.

MAR: So you see, if you disregard the pigeons—which you didn't like anyway—you have actually increased your possessions from 312 to 533.

ROD: But then, I lost some pretty big things too. After all, that bastard Guido the Provocative burned down one of my best castles.

MAR: On the other hand, however, in a reprisal raid you took from him the southern half of Wessex County.

ROD: I counted that. I added in a half for that.

MAR: That's just fine. You get half of Wessex and you lose 500 pigeons —so it's a net loss of 499½. As a matter of fact, the Guild is very worried about this. There is some nut—from Edinburgh, of course (wouldn't you know it)—who is going about the country advocating a new idea where you value everything and add it all up to a big total. Our Conduct and Discipline Committee think they can hang a witchcraft rap on him. This whole idea of his involves the introduction of new mathematical techniques—like long division. And of course the Guild feels that long division is too erratic and too subjective a process to be relied on for accounting. Our Research Committee have got out a pronouncement saying that they have considered the use of long division and have concluded that it is inappropriate at this time.

ROD: [*Shyly*] Do you think that your Guild would be interested in my idea of just counting things?

MAR: I'm afraid not. At best, they might endorse it as an alternative procedure, which is what they do when they want to go out of their way to be patronizing.

ROD: I do wish that Columbus would get going. When he discovers America, maybe we'll get some of these problems cleared up.

[*Curtain*]

Unfortunately, even the discovery of America has not resulted in our finding a satisfactory way to reach an appropriate cash equivalent for all assets. Moreover, as previously emphasized, this is not even the consistently acknowledged objective of the accountant. And until it is, progress towards better statements will be meagre.

The value for which we should be searching is a conversion value— that is to say, the amount of cash which an enterprise would be prepared to part with in order to acquire an asset if it did not own it, or the amount of cash which the enterprise would be prepared to accept for the asset if it did own it. In either case (purchase or sale), the amount of cash would be, if not identical, at least in the same target area—or near enough for our purposes.

Naturally, the calculation of such a value will inevitably involve some form of estimating procedure. One circumstance which has plagued accounting research is that accountants become so engrossed in procedures that they get to thinking about procedures even when they are trying to clarify their concept of value. Many fascinating procedures have been developed by accountants; but these are *methods* of obtaining objectives, and are not, in themselves, objectives. While trying to come to grips with our concept of value, we should forget about procedures. (This point is elaborated in Chapter 6, which deals with ground rules.)

It might be observed in passing that the case for current values has often bogged down on questions of refinements and procedures. For example, the cash equivalent of an asset may be taken as the cash price which the owner would accept for an asset—or, alternatively, as the amount of cash which a purchaser would be willing to part with in order to obtain the asset. Now, it can be argued that these might not necessarily be precisely the same figure. However, instead of becoming involved in an argument about which price we should use, it is better to remember the Keynesian principle that "it is better to be vaguely right than precisely wrong," and to conclude therefore that either of these values is acceptable—and leave it at that. The two approaches must yield substantially similar answers, and in the final analysis the choice between them is almost sure to be quite arbitrary.

Thus, the case for current values tends to get bogged down in an argument about procedures. We must thrash out our objectives at the outset and hence be quite clear about what we are trying to do. Questions of feasibility and of what procedures we should use are clearly of great importance—but a serious discussion of procedures should come later.

The Relationship Between Value and Income

It is necessary to digress here in order to consider the relationship between asset value and net-income determination. For many years, it has been common for accountants to claim that the income statement is more important than the balance sheet. This is true; and it is true partly because of the type of balance sheet that we issue. Composed as it is of a mixture of current and past costs, it is no wonder that the balance sheet is of limited use or interest. In fact, the tendency among accountants to divert attention to the income statement gives some indication of the recognized inadequacies of the balance sheet.

Actually, the income statement is very important—and there is nothing wrong with emphasizing this fact. A firm's net income is probably a better indication of its future strength (which is what most people want to know) than the net-asset position at any given date. (The nature of income will be considered more fully in the next chapter.) However, what we want to discuss at present is not whether the balance sheet or income statement is the more important statement. What we want to stress is that, if balance-sheet values are unsatisfactory, then by the same token the net-income figure will be unsatisfactory too—since net income includes the amortization of balance-sheet costs. Thus, if the balance sheet is not reliable, or if the picture it shows is distorted, then it follows that the income account must be similarly distorted. The balance sheet is important, not only in its own right, but also because the asset values in it eventually get written off against income.

The balance sheet and income statement are, in fact, best regarded as two parts of a single statement. Under double-entry principles (and double entry is, indeed, a beautiful invention), the earnings for a given period are established by comparing what is owned to start with and what is owned at the end—and the earnings are also established by comparing what is taken in during the period with what is paid out. Both calculations reach an identical conclusion. If one is right, then the other must be right; and if one is wrong, the other is too.

I will have more to say about income later; but for the moment, the point to note is this. Value is of crucial importance not only in the balance sheet; it is equally crucial in income determination. Anyone who suggests that the balance sheet is subject to criticism, but that this does not matter because income is properly stated, is just talking plain nonsense.

It is quite extraordinary what intellectual contortions some of our best pundits have gone through in an attempt to maintain that the balance sheet is *not* a valuation document. Since our professional exertions have, presumably, some rational objective, when we give up on the balance sheet, about the only thing that we can pretend to achieve is to measure income. But, if we measure income correctly (by matching revenues and costs, or by some such device), then surely the balance sheet (which represents the original contribution of capital plus accumulation of income less withdrawals) must correctly represent the residual value. If it does not, then the income must be wrongly stated—as there is presumably no room for argument about capital contributions or withdrawals.

Another exercise in futility is to assume that the investor's real interest in the assets of an enterprise lies in their earning power, and to argue from this that balance-sheet values should be arrived at by capitalizing income. How can we capitalize income without first determining what the income is? And how do we determine income without an appropriate amortization of asset values? To avoid this dilemma, it has been proposed that assets might be valued by capitalizing cash flow. But this would be worse still, since cash flow ties us more hopelessly than ever to transactions and ignores entirely the important non-transaction aspects in profit determination.

Problem Areas

Acceptance of the fact that each asset should be valued (as closely as may be) at the amount of cash which an enterprise would be willing to lay out to acquire it, is an essential first step on the road to better statements. But it is a step that is similar to Pilgrim's first step on his painful journey. Before we are finished, we shall pass through problem areas which will make the way through the Slough of Despond look like an eight-lane expressway. Converting assets to cash equivalent is not easy—it is simply necessary. No treatise of this sort can do justice to the difficulties that will arise; but some of the more obvious ones can be mentioned. The following paragraphs discuss the major problem areas.

1) *The "going concern" concept*

We certainly do not normally aim at liquidation values. Unless there are good reasons to the contrary, the natural assumption is that an enterprise will remain in business. We must start off, then, by assuming that accountants are correct in their adherence to the "going concern" principle. This is not always an easy concept to handle in practice. Moreover, the going concern theory must sometimes be abandoned—specifically, where an asset turns out to be worth more when it is diverted to some other use—as, for example, when a gold mine is discovered under the bunk house. The intention of the owners inevitably enters the calculation, and we must conclude that each asset should be valued on the basis of the use to which it is most likely to be committed. From this it follows that in highly exceptional circumstances the going concern concept should be abandoned.

2) *The eager beaver* versus *the reluctant dragon*

Determining the amount of cash that a company would exchange for an asset if it did not own it inevitably involves some kind of estimation. What we are groping for here is the price at which a hypothetical sale might be expected to go through. The catch is that in any sale, the price may depend to an important extent on the relative eagerness of the buyer to buy and of the seller to sell. Everyone knows that if a seller is desperate to sell, he will take less money—and that if a buyer is desperate to buy, he will pay more. Thus, reasonable estimates can cover a wide range, and of course this introduces a nasty element of uncertainty. This is not an easy problem. The important aim is fairness in determining where the valuation should be placed within the range of possibilities. Basically, we face here the question of the honesty of those who issue financial statements—and this is not a new problem. Whatever the principles used in preparing statements, good or bad judgment makes all the difference between informative and misleading presentations—and to a far greater extent than is usually supposed.

3) *Market uncertainties*

For certain types of assets there is a ready market, which greatly simplifies the valuation problem. Circumstances, however, vary greatly. Normally, marketable securities are fairly easy to value; but there are some problems. For example, the quantity of shares held may result in a market quotation's being somewhat misleading. The normal quoted market price is for exchanges of fairly standard board lots. A corporation with a very large holding may not be able to obtain anything like the market price, and this is a factor which may be important enough to require some recognition in the valuation process. Similarly, there are sometimes wide swings in price which could make the quotation on the balance-sheet date a poor indication of value. Thus, even for marketable securities (which represent about the simplest case imaginable) the valuation process is not always easy.

When we move to the valuation of inventories, we encounter much more difficult problems—problems of location, condition, etc. We may also encounter manufacturers', distributors', wholesale, and retail levels of prices. Thus, the valuation process can become quite complex. Nevertheless, the guiding principle remains the same: always attempt to establish a value at which the company would purchase the goods in normal quantities.

4) *Non-marketable goods*

For many goods, there is simply no market which provides current-price quotations. Somehow or other, these assets must be valued. What should be aimed at is their commercial value. This, of course, introduces many subjective considerations. It puts a very high premium on honesty. This kind of problem must sometimes be faced in court cases (where some definite decision must be reached) and the judge has to decide, as best he can, what a fair price would be in a transaction between a willing seller and a willing purchaser.

While there is no simple solution to the problem of determining current values where no market quotation is available, there are ways of tackling this difficulty. For example, by independent audit and other procedures, we can promote honesty in financial reporting and we can penalize dishonesty where it is discovered. Even when no market value can be reasonably estimated, there are, fortunately, other approaches. For example, there is no quoted market price for real estate, but there are usually similiar properties selling, from time to time, which give us some indication of current value. Similarly, by an appraisal of estimated construction costs, current values may be reached with some confidence for such difficult assets as buildings and heavy machinery.

Finally, in the midst of all our difficulties, it is right to remember that what we are seeking is not perfect and irreproachable valuations, but merely something better than a conglomeration of current costs, old costs, and market values. It may be a great comfort to a harassed accountant to be able to produce, in justification of his fixed-asset values, ancient documents which demonstrate that the asset once changed hands at the price he has used—but, once again, I would rather take my comfort in the old Keynesian refrain about it being better to be vaguely right than precisely wrong.

The "Fresh Start" Approach

The objective which must be always before us is to reach an honest commercial value—a value which can be defined, perhaps, in most general terms as that valuation which will start the corporation off with a clean slate in each financial period. The key notion is that we are dealing with period statements. A set of statements for the year ended June 30, 1969 should show what happened during that year. The general idea is to indicate to readers the success of the operation—a matter which is of interest to prospective investors, and also to shareholders who are considering the effectiveness of the management which they have appointed. The results of brilliant efforts in the past, or of mistakes in the past, should be equally ignored. For example, if the inventory is deemed to be excessive and it is expected that some price reductions will ultimately have to be made to move it, this fact should be recognized in valuing the inventory. The overpurchasing is a fault of management in past periods, and such periods should bear the cost of the mistakes. It would be wrong to bring the inventory in at a valuation which ignored the probability of price reductions and thus penalize the next period for past mistakes. Considerations of exactly the same kind apply in valuing other assets.

Assets Which Cannot Be Valued

There remains a further problem of great seriousness. This problem centers on the fact that the value of some perfectly good and valuable assets is not measurable at all. To put it more accurately, the assets which a business owns are measurable in differing degrees: some are easily and clearly measurable; others are only measurable by somewhat tenuous estimates and assumptions; and still others actually defy measurement.

It is not difficult to run an eye over a balance sheet and notice the variety of problems likely to be encountered. Since we define the valuation process as the establishing of a cash equivalent for different types of assets, there should presumably be no problem with cash, bank balances, overdrafts, and the like. Receivables present the relatively manageable problem of estimating collectability. Inventories, fixed assets, and intangibles pose more complicated difficulties—all of which will be discussed to some extent when we turn to consider procedures. All of these assets raise problems of varying difficulty under present accounting principles, and will also raise difficulties under current-value concepts. We should not expect to solve all such problems completely, but we should at least try to solve them as best we can.

An Interesting Opinion

Some encouraging support for the feasibility of asset measurement would seem to come from an AICPA Industry Audit Guide published recently (1968) with the title *Audits of Personal Financial Statements*. The committee which published this guide recommends that "financial statements for individuals should be prepared on a cost basis, in conformity with generally accepted accounting principles." It then goes on to state:

> The Committee recognizes that a disparity frequently exists between cost and estimated values. When the more common reasons for the use of personal financial statements are considered, it is evident that this disparity creates a need for a clear presentation of estimated values. For example, financial statements may be used for personal purposes, estate and income tax planning, contemplated retirement, credit purposes, and public disclosure by political candidates. In these situations, additional financial information on an estmiated value basis is useful.

The committee's notion of estimated value is simply what we have been calling current value, as can be seen from the following paragraph:

> "Estimated value" should represent fair market value in instances where it can be determined or reasonably estimated. Fair market value may be defined as the value determined by *bona fide* bargaining between well-informed buyers and sellers. In the case of closely held business interests, where fair market value is not ascertainable, cost adjusted for any accumulated undistributed earnings or losses since acquisition may be appropriate.

And the committee goes on to discuss various hard cases, making precisely the same kind of suggestions as are urged in later chapters of this text. It is interesting, too, to note that the committee also plays down the importance of standardized procedures for determining estimated value —as, for instance, when it says: "The methods of determining estimated value may vary from the date of one financial statement to another because of changed conditions and changes in available information.

Some change in the methods of determining estimated values may be necessary to present the best available estimates of current value." The committee naturally requires that such changes be disclosed.

Now all this refers to personal financial statements and not to the published statements of public corporations. But, for the life of me, I cannot see why information of estimated values should be less reliable or less useful in the case of statements issued by public corporations. The examples noted regarding the use of personal statements, which the committee puts forward as the reason for its recommendation, all apply (with the exception of political candidacy) to public corporations. And there are clearly even more important examples that would justify insistence on current values in the statements of such corporations.

In Summary

The important thing is to establish the principle that what we want is value-based statements. If this is accepted, then accountants can get down to work and find out how far they can go in valuing different types of assets. For some, an earnings approach may be feasible; but there will remain some assets which turn out to be quite unmeasurable. It will not, as a matter of fact, be a clear-cut matter of black and white. As suggested above, we can imagine ourselves tackling a range of assets classified in order of difficulty of valuation. As we move from one type of asset to the next, our valuations get more difficult, more tentative, and therefore less confident. We move from solid supporting data to more subjective criteria. As we proceed, there is more and more scope for honest differences of opinion. And if we are stubborn enough to push on along the scale of increasing difficulty of valuation, we eventually get to the point where our "valuations" are little more than wild guesses or figures pulled out of the air.

Any sensible person must realize that at some point in this process a halt should be called. We must say eventually: "This is as far as we should go." Beyond this point, assets are not measurable with sufficient reliability to justify the attempt. The point at which we stop must always be determined by good judgment and it will therefore be a matter of opinion. As in all similar accounting situations, this means that for published financial statements, the point at which we stop in our attempts to measure must be reached by "general acceptance"—which means, in turn, a consensus of the well-informed. (We shall return to this subject in Chapter 6.)

Our real objective, then, should be to do the best we can. It is entirely likely that the range of assets which can be measured satisfactorily will tend to be extended as new techniques are developed and as new equipment (notably computers) comes into use. We may then be able (by general consensus) to extend the scope of balance sheets and to take in types of assets which we have not at the moment found means of measuring reliably. Hopefully, we will get better and better statements as we progress. But the point on which it is absolutely essential that we reach agreement is that we should produce financial statements by measuring measurable assets as well as we possibly can. As this will leave some assets out of our reckoning entirely, the resulting statements will be incomplete and imperfect. But if we measure all measurable assets as well as they can be measured, we will at least produce much better statements than we do now.

In this review, some puzzling difficulties have emerged, and this is perhaps one of the most important advantages of the method recommended. It brings under scrutiny many of the shortcomings of modern statements, and this is better than sweeping them under the balance sheet. Hopefully, as a result of being exposed, they may eventually be solved. And if not, it is at least better to be aware of our shortcomings than to remain unaware of them.

CHAPTER 5

Income Determination

The figure that a person is most likely to look for in a set of financial statements is the amount of net income or net profits. To almost anyone who is interested in an enterprise, this is the key figure. An excess of assets over liabilities may be reassuring, and an excess of current assets over current liabilities is essential. But for most people, the really important thing is whether or not the company is profitable. No matter how strong its current position may be, if it is losing money, it will sooner or later be in trouble. As we have seen, a commercial enterprise can possess wealth and it can also possess the power to create it—with an established ability to earn, an enterprise can usually raise money either by borrowing or by issuing shares.

It follows from this that it is essential for accountants to develop a satisfactory concept of net income. We must remind ourselves again (since we keep forgetting this fact) that accounting is, pure and simple, a utilitarian discipline. We should not search for a concept of net income which is "true" or "logical," or which derives from some kind of basic reality. What we should look for is simply that concept of income which will prove most useful to those who are interested in determining the profit-earning capacity of an enterprise.

The Economics of Accounting

At this point, I must part company decisively with conventional concepts by insisting that the most useful picture of earnings is the picture which conforms most closely to the economic facts of life—that is, the picture which shows (as well as we can contrive to show it) how fast the economic wealth of the enterprise is growing (or is decreasing). We are dealing here with period statements, and the essential questions is this: By how much has the enterprise increased or decreased in value during a given period? I can imagine no other approach to the development of a proper income concept. It would be meaningless to claim that a company had made a net profit during a given period unless it could be demonstrated that its net assets had increased correspondingly. Otherwise, the natural question is surely this: If the enterprise has made a net profit of $1,000,000, where is the $1,000,000? In the preceding chapter, I spoke a bit harshly about those who admit that the balance sheet does not present a realistic picture, but who still claim that the income statement does. If the net-income statement establishes fairly and realistically how much has been earned, and if this is carried forward into a balance sheet which shows the accumulation of such earnings (along with capital contributions and withdrawals, about the accounting for which there is no argument), then the balance sheet must show an equally fair and realistic picture.

It would seem a safe conclusion that our concept of net income must be based on an increase in net assets—in other words, an increase in the value of the business from the beginning to the end of a given period. If this is accepted, then the task of producing an income statement boils down to the task of analysing the reasons for such increase and setting down the results of this analysis in the most informative manner possible.

Analysis of Growth

Let us consider the matter step by step:

1) We start with the fact that the net assets (valued as best we can value them) have increased during the period by a certain amount.

2) The first thing to do, then, is to distinguish between contributions of additional capital from outside and the growth of the enterprise through its operations; and we must naturally take account of withdrawals of both capital and earnings.

3) Once the so-called "capital" transactions have been eliminated, we are left with the amount by which the company has grown (or shrunk) otherwise. This amount has now to be analysed in order to demonstrate how much of the increase in value is due to monetary

factors (outside the control of the enterprise) and how much is due to the enterprise's own efforts. Here we encounter the distinction between *holding* profits and *operating* profits, a distinction which is fundamental. "Operating profit" is a concept familiar to accountants, and they have learned to handle it. It is simply a matter of recording income and of matching against it the expenditure which was made in earning it. The balance represents how much the enterprise has "earned." The second element of enhancement in value is the increases owing to inflation or monetary changes. These increases are called "holding" gains, since they accrue whether the company does anything or not.

4) The next step is to analyse net income from operations in order to explain how this income has occurred. In setting out to make such an analysis, one must remember that the important thing is to state the income (or increase in value) in terms which provide a basis for projecting future income. In a sense, past profits and losses are water over the dam. They have relevance or significance only as an indication of what may be expected to happen in the future. It follows from this that it is pointless to try to develop a concept of income on any assumption other than the assumption that future profits are what is important.

With this in mind, it becomes important to attempt, as far as this may be done, to distinguish normal operations from abnormal (or ordinary transactions from extraordinary) on the premise that the normal is more likely to recur than the abnormal. This explains the accountant's concern with the distinction between recurring and non-recurring profits (or, as we sometimes rather confusingly put it, between operating profits and capital profits). All such distinctions have the same object. In deciding how to analyse income into its basic elements, the important thing is to distinguish between regular earnings (which can be more or less counted upon, and which therefore form the basis for estimating what may happen in the future) and special items (which there is less reason to believe will recur).

The "Matching" Procedure

In developing our concept of income in the past, we have frequently used the method of matching income against the expenditure laid out to earn it. This practice has started us along the right track. Where we have gone wrong is in the area of holding profits and losses. Here, we have been quite illogical. What we have done, in effect, is to attempt to recognize holding *losses* while deliberately ignoring holding *gains*. Naturally, our concept of income is faulty to that extent. To argue otherwise is to say that the average statement-reader is interested when values move one way, but not when they move the other way. (As I shall argue in the following chapter, it is this wrong-headed treatment of holding gains and losses which has created the main difficulty when anyone has tried to draw up a satisfactory and generally acceptable code of accounting principles.)

An attempt is sometimes made to excuse this failure by pleading that valuation is a chancy and uncertain business. Well, sometimes it is and sometimes it isn't. But there is no reason to believe that downward revisions are any less difficult and any less risky than upward revisions. Usually, both are subject to the same uncertainties.

To make matters worse, accountants have not only confined their attention to holding losses, but have usually failed to distinguish the *holding* element from the *operating* element. Thus, a write-down of inventory when prices have fallen is not attributed to price-level changes, but instead gets inextricably lost in the inventory-valuation process. This results in less net profit being reported; but the statement-reader is usually left quite in the dark, since he has no way of knowing that the net profit would have been higher had it not been for a price drop. As such drops are usually beyond management's control, this is vital information to anyone who is trying to assess performance.

The Inclusive and Non-Inclusive Views of Earnings

Up to now, we have stressed the fact that net income is the all-important figure in a set of financial statements. It is on the basis of this figure that earning power is judged, since net income is the basis for projecting future profits and for calculating most of the important ratios, such as return on investment.

Inevitably, in discussing net income, we must become involved in problems of semantics. In defining "net income," the accounting profession has tended to vacillate between the view that net income should cover only normal earnings and the view that net income should cover all earnings made—whether these earnings be ordinary or extraordinary. Thus arises the debate between the so-called *inclusive* and *non-inclusive* definitions of earnings. In this debate, there are valid arguments on both sides. The inclusive view states that anyone who carries on business must inevitably encounter certain profits or losses that are not, strictly speaking, in the normal course of business; and since all companies nevertheless make such profits or losses, these should be included in net income. For example, a non-investment enterprise may often operate in such a way that it has, from time to time, surpluses of cash on hand which are temporarily invested in marketable securities. Thus, the enterprise may earn profits (or make losses) on these temporary investments. The non-inclusive view regards these as extraneous, and would eliminate them when calculating net income. On the other hand, the inclusive view would include such profits on the grounds that they are a normal feature of the enterprise's operation—even though they have not been earned in the pursuit of the corporation's main line of business.

This problem is further complicated by the existence of situations in which it is difficult to decide what an enterprise's main line of business really is. Take, for example, insurance companies. It is a normal part of the operations of insurance companies to accumulate funds which form a permanent investment portfolio. Thus, an insurance company may operate quite successfully with consistent underwriting losses on its insurance business, but high profit from its investment transactions. That this is not unusual may be gleaned from the fact that an analysis of the combined financial results of all fire and casualty companies in the United States over a 45-year period indicated that they had earned $3 billion in underwriting profits while earning $6 billion in investment revenue and making $9 billion in net profit on the sale of securities. If we start excluding things from net-income determination, we may find it very difficult to know where to draw the line.

In the end, however, this problem is not really a matter of life and death, and we are perhaps doing little more than playing with words. So long as extraneous profits and losses are segregated and shown separately, it is hard to pretend that it matters very much whether they are taken into income before or after the figure of net income is struck. The question that emerges, then, is this: Is the term "net income" more appropriately applied to the net of the "normal" items, or is it more useful to use this term to distinguish the final balance after the so-called extraneous items have been taken into consideration? Clearly, both figures are of use to us. It is simply a matter of reaching a general agreement (or consensus) on what we will call net income. The other significant balance, which is not called "net income," would simply have to be christened something else.

So far as I can see, the question is satisfactorily settled in the *Hand-*

book of The Canadian Institute of Chartered Accountants, which says:

> The Research Committee has concluded that net income should reflect all gains or losses recognized during the period except prior period adjustments and capital transactions. The Committee has also concluded that it is essential to distinguish extraordinary items contributing to net income.[4]

In other words, extraordinary items should be taken into consideration in arriving at the amount of the net income—but should be shown as a separate item. The *Handbook* goes on to define "extraordinary" in the following terms:

> Extraordinary items may be defined as material gains or losses which are not typical of the company's normal business activities, are not expected to occur regularly over a period of years, and are not considered as recurring factors in any evulation of the ordinary operating processes of the business.[5]

This definition would exclude from the "extraordinary" classification any large or unusual gains and losses which occur in the company's general line of activity—all of which is fair enough.

Prior-Year Adjustments

A further element that enters into the difference between net-asset value at one year end and the next, is the prior-year items which frequently arise. For example, in calculating income tax liability (under Canadian practice at least), a corporation is obligated to calculate its own tax, subject to later assessment by the tax department. In a corporation of any size, there are inevitably many items of a debatable nature—for example, receipts which may or may not be deemed taxable, and expenditures which may or may not be allowed as deductions. The financial statements of a corporation have always to be issued long before the tax department has had an opportunity to complete its assessment, and in fact usually before the corporation has filed its tax return. It is therefore very common to encounter prior-year tax adjustments—which are credits or debits which must be taken up in the accounts of the current financial year, but which have no application to it. They are simply adjustments of the taxable income declared in previous years. Where these are significant, they must be segregated, if a reasonably comprehensible picture is to be provided.

4. Section 3480.02   5. Section 3480.03

In Summary

Perhaps we can summarize the classifications which are required in analysing changes in net-asset value as follows:

1. Contributions and withdrawals of capital.
2. Withdrawals of accumulated income (dividends).
3. Holding gains and losses resulting from such external circumstances as changes in the general price level, foreign exchange fluctuations, and so on.
4. Ordinary income and expenditure of the company.
5. Extraordinary items of profit or loss not in the normal line of business.
6. Adjustments of prior-year income.

A great deal of additional analysis can be done (and will in fact be needed) to make the statement more meaningful. For example, the ordinary income of a large modern corporation usually consists of very diverse elements, and such conglomerate figures as total sales may well be a mish-mash of diverse items. Clearly, an analysis of revenue on the basis of main products is an elementary requirement in many situations. On the expenditure side, the corresponding cost might be segregated to produce "gross profit" by product lines.

Beyond this point, it is difficult to generalize. The basic idea must always be to distinguish the important categories of revenues and expenses; but which categories might be adjudged suitable depends on the nature of the business. Labour, purchases of supplies, taxes, selling expenses, and administrative expenses are popular classifications. However, none of them are sacred.

"Realization"

In dealing with the income statement, it is necessary to consider the "realization concept" which has been a cardinal dogma in accounting. This concept is the result of an attempt to meet the problems of producing periodic statements. For such statements, increases and decreases in asset value must be definitely allocated to a specific period of time. Sometimes (perhaps in most cases), this is a simple matter. If, within a given financial period, certain goods are bought and sold, it is difficult not to conclude that the total proceeds from the sale and the total cost of the goods and the expenses of handling them, should all be included within the period in question. The problem arises when transactions are not complete within one period—as, for example, when goods are purchased in one period, carried forward in the inventory at the year end, and sold in a subsequent period. The expenses in this case have to be allocated between two periods—namely, the year of purchase and the year of sale. And when you come right down to it, this allocation must be done on an arbitrary basis—since no logical basis is available. Similarly, a building that is put up in one period and is in service over many subsequent periods presents a problem in allocation of cost.

In coping with these admittedly difficult subjects, accountants have developed certain rules or "principles" which they call the "realization concept." It was to be expected that a set of cautious rules would be developed, and the result is a concept which is basically intended (although it has been in force so long that few accountants may now appreciate or admit it) to protect accountants as much as possible from any charge of misleading people. The general idea emerged that profits should be deferred as long as possible. This is a fine system for someone who wants to be sure that no one can ever accuse him of painting too glowing a picture, but it is a ridiculous system for one who is trying to produce financial statements which will provide fair and impartial information—that is, statements which will prove equally usable by buyers and sellers, and by lenders and borrowers.

Many distortions can arise from the accountant's concept of realization. For example, marketable securities are normally carried at cost unless they drop in value. This means that an investment held, say, over twenty years in a rising market will not show any profit until it is finally sold. When it is finally sold, it will show, in the final year of sale, a profit which has accumulated over twenty years. This makes absolutely no sense.

If we are to produce sensible statements, we must completely scrap the realization theory which we have cherished for so long. It is simply a bundle of arbitrary rules-of-thumb which may have made sense when they were first invented, but which have long since ceased to be useful. For instance, in the case of marketable securities mentioned above, if the book value was adjusted to market value at the end of each year (and this is not a formidable task), the statements would show clearly the amount by which the value of the securities had altered during each year. What else should we be trying to do?

CHAPTER 6

Generally Accepted
Accounting Ground Rules

. . . the standards of the accounting profession . . . are not derivable from physical science or natural law; they are, rather, conventions, related to certain necessarily pragmatic postulates, whose existence and validity derive from public exposure, debate, and acceptance. Generally accepted accounting principles, . . . in short, are not discovered, but declared. Their existence cannot forerun their utterance and acceptance by the profession itself.[6]

In the world of accounting there is certainly nothing more frustrating, more conducive to troubled conscience, or more time-wasting than arguments about our generally accepted principles. I have always claimed that we have, in point of fact, a fairly well organized set of principles to subscribe to. One accountant can never expect to encounter all the difficult situations that might conceivably arise, but in over thirty years of practice I have faced a considerable variety of problems—and I can hardly remember a case in which there was much doubt about what accounting principle should be applied. Every time a set of audited statements is published, some auditor must give his solemn professional opinion as to whether or not the statements conform to generally accepted principles; and the auditors (a notably conscientious lot) do not seem to have any trouble in making the necessary affirmation. If they had any doubts as to just what the principles were, this certainly would not be the case.

6. From an *amicus curiae* brief submitted by The American Institute of Chartered Accountants in a 1968 law case.

After all, in a general sort of way it's all pretty obvious. Assets sort themselves out into a few familiar groupings. Current assets are stated at market, or at the lower of cost and market. Other assets are usually stated originally at cost—which is either carried forward indefinitely (as in the case of land), or written off systematically (as in the case of other tangible fixed assets), or treated in almost any way you like (as in the case of some of the intangibles). Similarly, everyone knows more or less what a liability is, and a few fairly simple general rules of income recognition have been evolved. Moreover, adequate disclosure of what has been done will usually get you off the hook in cases where there is doubt. That's about all there is to it—until you sit down to write all this out a bit more formally and precisely. Then the heavens fall in.

Let us go back to the beginning and try to determine why it has proved impossible to write a satisfactory code when everyone more or less agrees what should be in it.

The Necessity of Consensus

Financial statements are essentially conventional. There is no alternative to this; they simply could not be prepared in any other way. If I am right in insisting that we should build our accounting on current values, it is not because there is any intrinsic merit in such a proposal. It is because statements that are produced on this basis would be more useful to the generality of users than the statements which we now issue.

If we are to have a really satisfactory consensus, we must not merely agree, in a vague sort of way, on what we are trying to achieve. We should also be able to state clearly and in considerable detail what it is that we are agreeing upon. Hence the necessity of drawing up a code.

It has been customary, in this context, to speak of "principles." But to my mind, this implies too awesome an authenticity. I think that the term "conventions" is more appropriate. To make the true nature of our pronouncements unmistakably apparent, I have even some fondness for the term "ground rules." In short, it is accepted ground rules that we want.

Drafting a Code

The task of drafting a code has received a great deal of attention from the profession; and a number of attempts at a code, as explained previously, have been produced by textbook authors and institute committees. But the whole subject has produced such a pall of frustration that one could easily conclude, from listening in on accounting discussions, that nothing has ever been accomplished.

It is my conviction that no satisfying code can be produced until we change our basic concept from cost to current valuation. To repeat my line of reasoning once more: our present approach is basically illogical, and we cannot build a satisfactory code on an illogical base. Contrariwise, I believe that if we do accept the logic of current values, a satisfactory code could be produced.

In saying this, I do not intend to minimize the difficulty of the task —I only predict that it would be possible. After all, this would constitute some degree of progress—the possible being quite an improvement on the impossible.

The fleshing out of the broad generalizations that we have been dealing with in this text will take a great deal of time and thought. But our accounting art will never be in a completely satisfactory state until such general ideas as current value have been elaborated upon and clear rules have been made available to (and comprehensible by) those who are responsible for producing financial statements.

In attempting to write a code, we will have to remember that a pragmatic art, such as accounting, is not susceptible to the rigid legal-type draftsmanship which is feasible (and necessary) in writing statutory law. The admirable handbook issued recently (December 1968) by The Canadian Institute of Chartered Accountants has this to say:

> . . . the Committee [of Accounting and Auditing Research] recognizes that no rule of general application can be phrased to suit all circumstances or combination of circumstances that may arise, nor is there any substitute for the exercise of professional judgment in the determination of what constitutes fair presentation or good practice in a particular case.[7]

This is well said. It emphasizes the fact that even a written code of generally accepted rules will have to be stated in broad terms. The object can only be to explain, as clearly as possible, the intentions or aims of statement-producers—rather than to provide meticulous directions which are meant to be strictly interpreted in preparing statements.

A Distillation from Practice

Our code of ground rules will always be a distillation from practice. This is inevitable in an art that is subject to constant change. Refinements of

7. From the preface to the *Handbook of The Canadian Institute of Chartered Accountants.*

rules and new methods of coping with problems should emerge from the practical work of actually issuing statements, the written code being brought up to date as the art develops.

A good many terms get bandied about when accountants talk of their art—terms like "postulates," "principles," "conventions," "methods," "rules," and "procedures." But I have never been convinced that we need more than two categories. Let us call these categories "ground rules" and "procedures." The distinction between ground rules and procedures I hold to be of absolutely capital importance. This is the basic distinction between *what* we are trying to achieve (ground rules) and *how* we are trying to achieve it (procedures).

Accounting would be a disorganized shambles if we did not have a reasonably clear-headed consensus on *what* we are trying to do. This is what belongs in our code. On the other hand, I can see no particular merit in standardizing procedures. I think, in fact, that attempts to do so have only served to confuse the whole issue. In my opinion, an insistence on standardized procedures is wholly unrealistic—even if it could be achieved, it would be undesirable. I believe that if we agree clearly on the ground rules, then procedures can be left to look after themselves. I would like now to quote what I have said (I think with some lucidity) on another occasion:

> To hear accountants talk, one might gather that uniformity of procedures was about the most important problem we have. But how real is the problem? To take a simple example, suppose that of three competing manufacturers, one has a plant that was built in 1964, another a plant that was built in 1950, and the third a plant that was built in 1920. There is no reason in either logic or common sense that requires each of these companies to value its plant by the same procedure. Once the current-value concept is accepted, it becomes quite unnecessary to insist that all three competitors estimate their plant values by the same processes, so long as each of them uses the method which, in its case, will provide the closest estimate to current value. For instance:
>
> i) The company with the 1964 plant might best value its plant at original cost. Unless there is some extraordinary reason to the contrary, the company would probably replace this plant (if it were detroyed) by a substantially similar type of building at a substantially similar cost. Of course, if there were some extraordinary reason that made this inappropriate, some other approach might be required. But normally, original cost should be quite satisfactory in a case like this.
>
> ii) The company with the 1950 plant might find that it could best reach an appropriate current value by appraisal. Construction costs have changed considerably since 1950 and a somewhat different type of

building might be built today. Original cost in these circumstances
starts to become unsatisfactory.

iii) The company with a 1920 plant might conclude that the best way
to represent the present value of its plant would be to estimate the
cost of a modern factory of similiar usable floor space.

Surely there can be little virtue in insisting that two of the three companies must adopt an unsatisfactory method of valuing their plant, simply
to have the three competing companies use the same basis. Comparability
is achieved because the three companies are all using methods that are
aimed at the same result. What is important is what they achieve (i.e.,
the closest approach to current value that is practicable) and not that
they all reach their asset values by identical techniques.

It is important to realize that precisely the same consideration would
apply if one company owned all three plants. There would still be no
reason to use anything but the best valuation method in each case.

Important considerations inevitably tend to get glossed over in generalized discussion. Let me illustrate. A questionnaire once sent around
by the Canadian Tax Department included the following item: "Describe how your inventory is valued." Most corporations solemnly
answered this question with some phrase such as: "At the lower of cost
or market; first in, first out." This answer apparently satisfied the corporation executives supplying the information and also the tax department. And yet, for a large modern corporation, an answer of this sort
has to be silly. Any large modern corporation has an enormous variety
of inventories, and one general approach to all of them would be unthinkable. One corporation answered the tax department's questionnaire
as follows: "Our corporation has a great variety of inventories. In
attempting to reach a reasonable value for them, we use every method
of inventory valuation we have ever heard of, and a few we have invented ourselves. The only thing that can be safely said is that, for each
type of inventory, we use the method of valuation that seems most
appropriate, and we use a consistent basis for each class of goods from
year to year."

One must remember that the inventory of a large corporation
typically includes goods of such diversity as French pastries, used farm
equipment, high-fashion gowns, electronic devices, diamonds, and so on.
It would be ridiculous to attempt to impose a rigid approach to inventory valuation even within one corporation—let alone throughout a
whole industry or over corporations generally.

There is nothing wrong with research into the best inventory
methods for different types of goods. But it makes little sense to start out
with the assumption that there is any merit in seeking one basis which
will apply to all types of goods.[8]

In my view, the concern for standardization of procedures arises
from the fact that we do not have logical principles. We lack a logical
set of principles because we have dealt *ad hoc* with difficulties as they

8. From the Berkeley Symposium on "The Foundation of Financial Accounting, January 1967.

have arisen. This has meant the sanctioning of arbitrary adjustments—and, groping around for some way of bringing order into our discipline, we have tried to achieve standardization of the permitted adjustments to cost. If we once moved to a logical base such as current values, it seems to me that we could stop worrying about standard procedures.

Legal Sanction

Perhaps it is well to dispose of the notion that accounting rules can be codified by following legal precepts as embodied in statutes or judgments. In the early days of serious financial reporting (say at the start of the nineteenth century), great interest was taken in financial reporting by jurists. The joint stock company was in the process of being developed (ultimately leading to the limited liability corporation) and this fascinating invention at first prompted a good deal of activity in the courts, when learned judges gave decisions in accounting matters which are still quoted. However, the jurists concentrated mainly on the problem of determining what profits were available for payment of dividends. The daring new concept of limited liability opened the door to a variety of direct and simple-minded frauds based on the owners' drawing out their stakes—to the ruination of creditors. Such questions as the amount of dividends that should be permitted became contentious, and their Lordships wrestled manfully with abstruse matters such as the distinction between fixed capital and circulating capital.

These cases are still of some intellectual interest, but they have very little practical relevance to the problems of current accounting. Public corporations in North America normally finance themselves, to a very large extent, by retained earnings. There is little observable tendency to increase dividends to the ultimate legal limit. The crooked company promoter has moved on to more sophisticated kinds of skullduggery than the payment of unearned dividends. The question of whether or not surplus (or "retained earnings," as we have come to describe it) is available for dividends thus tends to be somewhat academic.

From time to time, company law is brought up to date, the clauses dealing with financial statements being brought into line with good current practice. This is the proper sequence. It must be the legal requirements which follow the code (that code having been worked out in practice) and not the other way around. Whatever the difficulties of reaching a consensus among accountants, these difficulties are inevitably less than the ponderous procedure of drafting statutes and piloting them through the legislature. Pronouncements from the Bench can be helpful (or troublesome), but they deal with specific points raised in litigation. They cannot be expected to cover the whole field of accounting in a systematic way.

Thus, our legal brethren cannot contribute effectively to the building up of an accounting code. The most that we can hope for is that they will follow it, once it is written, when making legal pronouncements or drafting legislation.

Arriving at a Consensus

The fact that accounting has to be based on a consensus of opinion leads us immediately to other questions, such as:

> 1) Who should make the decisions?
> 2) Who should be included in the consensus?
> 3) Should votes be counted or weighed?
> 4) How are conflicting views of the accountant, the analyst, and others to be reconciled?

Attempts so far to state generally accepted accounting ground rules have encouraged the idea that it might be possible to get a firm meeting of the minds of all those varied groups which are interested, in one way or another, in financial statements. This would naturally be desirable. However, we encounter here natural limitations on what is possible. As one authority puts it: "If one consults a sufficiently large number of people for a long enough time, one can develop insurmountable opposition to the most innocuous idea." [9]

While it would be nice to get everyone in on the act (if this were practicable), we will never get a code drafted unless we limit participation. Even without consulting statement-users at all, accounting bodies who have attempted to draw up generally accepted principles have encountered great difficulty in getting unanimity (or even substantial agreement) in making pronouncements. Bodies like The Canadian Institute of Chartered Accountants or The American Institute of Certified Public Accountants, who have been trail-blazers in this field, have found they have had to delegate the task of making pronouncements to relatively small groups of members—groups chosen in the hope that they

9. Quoted by H. V. Dodds, in *The American President: Education or Caretaker?* New York, 1962, p. 108.

might comprise a fairly representative cross-section of the profession. Attempts to have the resulting pronouncements endorsed by the full membership, or even by the councils of these institutes, have demonstrated how difficult it is to get a really broad consensus.

The fact remains that if accounting is to be based on a consensus, then someone must take the responsibility for providing one—and the accounting institutes are the logical places to look for leadership. If not there, where else? The institutes must be the logical custodians of the art of accounting. They represent a group of people whose existence is justified only if they conduct their affairs in the public interest, professionally, with a maximum degree of independence. Robert M. Trueblood, a past president of the AICPA, has put the matter this way:

> No one can deny that standards of financial accounting are essential in our society. It is not only logical but, in my estimation, imperative that these standards be set by the Institute—and that means the APB [the Accounting Principles Board].
>
> This is so, I believe, because there is no other non-government agency that can do the job. And certainly no thoughtful person, familiar with the problems, would be happy to have government undertake the job. Accountants would not be pleased with such a solution. Business certainly would not be. And, according to statements of its spokesmen over the years, the SEC would not desire to have the assignment thrust upon it. Industry itself is not organized to assume the task of defining accounting principles and procedures. Although individual corporate managements may sometimes object to specific conclusions of the APB, I firmly believe that management as a group will be glad to have the accounting profession shoulder the primary responsibility in this matter.[10]

Every time a pronouncement comes out that stipulates a ground rule which someone disagrees with, or that requires a disclosure which someone does not wish to make, there is apt to be criticism of the institutes. "Who do they think they are, chucking their weight about?" But the fact remains that someone has to make decisions. A general consensus of everyone would be impossible. If the accounting institutes do not undertake this difficult and thankless task, then government regulatory bodies will be forced to draft the rules themselves. They are not actually well equipped to do so; and it is to the everlasting credit of those who run such agencies in countries like Canada, the United States, and England, that they have appreciated this fact and have, as far as possible, allowed the professional institutes to do the job. However, unless these institutes do the job properly, it will eventually have to be done by mandatory government regulation—much to the detriment of everybody.

10. From remarks made to the Council of the AICPA, May 1966.

The User Point of View

Almost inevitably, the responsibility for making pronouncements must devolve upon the professional institutes—for the several reasons given above. Moreover, in deciding upon ground rules, the institutes should strive to serve the best interests of all statement-users. These interests, however, are not easy to assess. The straightforward approach of asking users what information they would like has not been as fruitful as one might expect it to be. It seems logical enough to determine what people want simply by *asking* them what they want. But the trouble is that users are often not in a position to decide what they want, because they are not fully aware of the range of information with which they can be supplied. If, in the last century, trans-Atlantic travellers in sailing ships had been asked what improvements they would like in means of travel, presumably they could not have been expected to call for the jet airliner —and yet this is precisely the improvement that did eventually develop. This analogy will be carried further later. For the moment, it is enough for us to notice that while institutes should have the responsibility for laying down ground rules, they must act in the best interest of users.

The Seat of Responsibility

There is one terribly important point about financial reporting that seems to have been quite generally overlooked. That point is simply this: if we are to have satisfactory statements, they must be statements prepared on ground rules which are understandable to the decision-makers who use them, as well as to the professional accountants who prepare them.

In the past, arguments about accounting principles have been largely confined to discussions between professionals—and the professionals have devoted their time to debating technicalities. But if better statements are ever to be produced, people who are not accountants must get into the act—and getting into the act implies understanding the issues. These "others" are not the "average shareholder"—i.e., the widow or the orphan, characters dear to the heart of the public relations expert turned financial critic. Their place is on the sidelines, and their interests should be looked after by those who are trained to protect the unknowledgeable. The non-accountants who must have serious responsibilities for financial statements are the company directors and those members of the management team who are involved in making basic decisions, but who have not had a professional accounting training. To appreciate how important this is in establishing our accounting code, it is necessary to consider, a little more closely, the process by which statements are prepared and issued.

We are considering only those statements of public corporations which are prepared for submission to shareholders. We talk of such statements as being prepared "by management" or "by the company." However, these simple phrases gloss over an extremely complicated process. To begin with, the bits and pieces which will ultimately be integrated into the final confection start being worked on in departments scattered throughout the corporation. Some of this preliminary work is in the hands of accounting types—for example, the summarization and analysis of the cash and bank transactions. But other work is contributed by members of the staff who do not have accounting backgrounds—members such as the credit staff (who help in assessing the collectability of receivables) or the production men (who assess the physical condition of the inventory). These varied and scattered activities must be controlled and drawn together by a responsible official. This official may operate under any one of several different titles (controller, treasurer, vice-president finance) and we may describe him as the "chief financial officer." Up to this point, while an assortment of non-accountants may have played important parts in preparing the statements, there is a final review by a responsible officer, who, we may assume, has a good technical grasp of the accounting process.

Before the statements are issued, they must go through a final stage of approval, and this final review is of absolutely vital importance. In Canada, it is standard corporate practice that the annual statements are prepared by management and ultimately approved for issue by the board of directors. The board has, thus, the ultimate responsibility for the statements. As I understand it, this is generally the situation elsewhere.

The functions of a board of directors are sometimes not too clearly understood. Encouraged, perhaps, by the popular form of corporate organization chart (which shows the board at the top with lines of authority leading down through the chief executive officer), some people think of the board as the top management authority of the company. But the basic responsibility of the board is not to manage the company; its basic responsibility is to see that it is well managed—and that is quite another matter. It is, then, the most obvious task of the board to see that good management is selected and retained, or (if it turns bad) changed. To do this effectively, the board must maintain continuous supervision of management's performance; and this, in turn, means that the board should insist on the best system of financial reporting that can possibly be devised. Anyone who has dabbled in this area will have found out how difficult management supervision really is (even in the best of circumstances) and will realize that it is the duty of the board to insist on the clearest communication of information.

It follows, therefore, that the board of directors must inevitably be concerned about accounting principles. It is not only that they require significant data in order to perform their essential function of keeping an eye on management; but they must also take the responsibility of approving the statements which are submitted to the shareholders as management's report on its stewardship. Clearly, they cannot carry out this responsibility properly unless they have assured themselves that the statements present as fair and as reasonable an account of what has happened as can be produced. The only way in which they can assure themselves of this is by comprehending the basis on which the statements have been prepared.

Let us now return to the process of statement production. So far, we have followed the gathering of basic data from various sources and its integration into financial statements (here we should say *draft statements*) under the control and supervision of the chief financial officer. These draft statements then go to the chief executive officer, who has the top management responsibility and who may operate under any one of a number of different titles—chairman, president, general manager, managing director. This post may be filled by a man who has a professional accounting background; but there are many roads to the top, and the chances are therefore against it. At any rate, whether or not the chief executive officer has an accounting background, once he is satisfied with the statements, he must present them to his directors—very few of whom are likely to have had a technical accounting training, although they will normally have had wide business experience.

We come now to the crux of the matter. It is most unlikely that better financial statements will be published unless the company directors, who have the final responsibility for issuing them, understand the principles at stake. We must reluctantly banish the Utopian idea of a world run entirely by professional accountants, and the only other solution is to build a code of accounting principles which can be understood by men who do not have a thorough technical background in accounting. Our code need not be produced at a level which is comprehensible to a person who is completely inexperienced in business; but it must be capable of being understood by any experienced executive with a good general business background. After all, this is the sort of fellow for whom the statements are being prepared—and if he does not understand them, what good are they?

It is here, I think, that the accounting profession has gone astray. For we have tried to construct our accounting principles on technical concepts which we understand and which nobody else does. And no amount of sophisticated refinement will get us back on the right trail. It may seem strange to those who are steeped in the subject, but the fact remains that few people who are not accountants can understand our depreciation procedures. The typical director has an uneasy feeling that there is something arbitrary and not quite real about the depreciation charge; and if the discussion gets around to the difference between depreciation booked and depreciation claimed for tax purposes, he tends to withdraw and to leave the matter to the accountants. There are many other important points at which accountants have sought technical refinements of their concepts, rather than devising the common-sense sort of rules which intelligent businessmen could aspire to understand without taking a course in the technicalities of statement production. To take just one more example: in the crucial area of inventory valuation, we find the rule of "the lower of cost and market"—a rule which sounds simple enough until you get down to the intricacies of what is "cost" and what is "market."

By following statement production through its various stages, and by recognizing that ultimate responsibility must rest on a board which is not likely to be composed of trained accountants, we may appreciate from yet another angle the logic of current values. You do not have to have enjoyed the benefits of a technical training in accounting to understand the principle of determining your wealth by valuing what you own and deducting what you owe. Nor is it necessary to grasp the intricacies of statement production in order to appreciate that you should report, as net profit for the year, the amount by which your wealth has increased during the year. A code of accounting ground rules based on these simple and self-evident premises could be understood by any sensible laymen. And this is the sort of code that we must have if directors are ever to be able to play their essential role effectively.

Observe how fundamental this point is. The most important single step in financial-statement production should be the final approval of the statements, by the board of directors, for publication—although you would never suspect this from the way it usually comes off in practice. This should be a solemn moment; because those who are ultimately responsible for the statements are deciding whether or not the statements communicate the essential facts about the enterprise, fairly and clearly, for the use of those who have reason to know what is going on.

Let us consider the position in which a good, well-chosen director finds himself on such an occasion. Mr. Alright is honest, fair-minded, and conscientious; he is also intelligent and experienced. He wants, moreover, to do his job well. But he has not had professional accounting training. Therefore, on technical accounting questions, he must rely to a large extent on others.

Under present accounting principles, Mr. Alright has very little opportunity to make an intelligent contribution to the discussion of the annual financial statements. He is most likely to confine himself to finding out whether or not the officers or directors who do have an accounting background are satisfied. If he makes any remark, other than to satisfy himself that those in whom he has confidence are satisfied, the conversation is likely to go something like this:

ALRIGHT: I see that our plant is in at $10,000,000. Surely it must be worth much more than that?

PRESIDENT: Oh, of course it is.

ALRIGHT: Well, why then do we say that it is worth $10,000,000?

PRESIDENT: Because we built most of it when costs were much lower, we received various government incentive grants, and we have been writing it down at the maximum rates of depreciation allowable.

ALRIGHT: Why do we do all this if it ends up with reporting the value of our plant at a figure that is obviously lower than it is?

PRESIDENT: It isn't really a matter of value. Under accepted accounting principles, the correct way to state plant is at cost less depreciation. It is not considered right to recognize value increases until these are unequivocally established by an actual arm's length sale. There is some leeway in the method used in writing off cost; but as a matter of common prudence, we believe in using the most conservative procedures that are allowed under generally accepted practice.

ALRIGHT: All right then.

Under present principles, what else can Mr. Alright say? But see how different the whole discussion might have been if our principles had been based on current values. In such case, our principles would be understandable to an intelligent director even though he was not an accountant. Thus, the approval of the financial statements by the board could be a genuine approval, and not merely a process in which the majority of those present had simply to assume that certain financial officers knew what they were doing. Under such conditions, you could imagine conversations going more like this:

ALRIGHT: I see that our plant is in at $20,000,000. Surely it must be worth much more than that?

PRESIDENT: We don't think so. The $20,000,000 is the value reached by Knowledgeable Appraisers Inc. and it seems reasonable to us. They took land in at $15 a square foot, for example.

ALRIGHT: But isn't that too low? I thought Neighbours Limited sold that land next door for $25 a foot last January.

PRESIDENT: That's true. But the appraisers felt that that sale should be ignored, as it was part of an elaborate exchange deal which could have influenced the price. They point out that more recently several properties in this area have gone through at around $15.

ALRIGHT: What about buildings?

PRESIDENT: Well, they too were appraised by Knowledgeable. Basically, they used a cubic content approach. We've been over their figures and think them reasonable. Here, for example, is their report. Let's just have a look at their assumptions on cubic content values.

This sort of conversation could go on and on. The point is that under present conditions, there is no possibility of an intelligent discussion by non-accountants. In current-value accounting, on the other hand, an intelligent discussion could easily take place—since our code of principles would not be a jumble of technical conventions that are designed to make an apparently logical system out of basically false premises. In short, current values present a goal which is understandable because it corresponds to the goal which we should actually have.

The responsibility of directors is truly awesome. And the tendency seems to be towards insisting more and more strongly on this responsibility. If we are to persist in holding individuals so onerously responsible, surely we must provide them with a reporting system which they have some hope of understanding.

The Development of a Consensus

What is implied by the term "general acceptance"? It implies a consensus of opinion, but this is rather vague. To make precise, strictly-enforceable rules would require some sort of clear-cut authority—and general acceptance is much too vague a concept to form a basis for such mandatory rules. Out of a general consensus of opinion can only come the sort of rules which are adhered to because they make clear, good sense. In this respect, the analogy with grammar has always seemed enlightening to me. Textbooks on English grammar can stir up all sorts of arguments. But it must surely be conceded that there is, nevertheless, some sort of general consensus as to what is good grammar and what is bad. Our rules of grammar have evolved slowly and naturally from a study of the better authors, and our general consensus in accounting must inevitably develop in much the same way—that is to say, as a distillation from the better statements that are produced.

If the ground rules of accounting can develop from practice, as do our rules of grammar, it might be wondered why any group (such as an institute committee) needs to be set up to make pronouncements. Why not let accounting rules develop naturally from precedent to precedent—as in the case of English grammar? The difference, here, is really one of urgency. Through the centuries, we have acquired a reasonably well-developed consensus on grammar. But accounting is a much newer enterprise and involves rapidly-changing circumstances which make the automatic emergence of sound rules, by a sort of Darwinian process of survival of the fittest, much too slow and uncertain a process. For example, the invention of the computer has completely revolutionized the type of information that can be made available, and consequently our use of the computer will profoundly alter our concepts of financial reporting. When developments of such suddenness occur, the natural growth of accounting conventions from accounting practice must be supplemented by deliberate and conscious attempts to speed up the process.

To sum up, the responsibility for providing leadership in developing an accounting code is best left to the institutes of accountants. While the necessary machinery should be developed under the auspices of the institutes, it would nevertheless be helpful if the group which is charged with the task of producing pronouncements was as broadly based as possible —including, for example, representatives of management, investment analysts, and perhaps members of the staff of regulatory bodies. The balance of representation is a matter of detail. The main objective would be to get as broad a group as possible while still assuring the emergence of well-supported conclusions. Moreover, the code must not be simply a compilation of technical provisions; its terms must be broadly understandable by the important groups who use the statements and who have ultimate legal and moral responsibility for issuing them.

Content of an Accounting Code

As I have already said, I believe that if current-value accounting is once accepted, the problem of producing a satisfactory statement of generally accepted ground rules will prove soluble. The precise working-out of the code will be a major undertaking, but perhaps it is not too difficult to surmise the sort of content which the code might be expected to have.

A great deal of clear thinking and good writing went into a report by a study group of the American Accounting Association that was published in 1966 under the title of *A Statement of Basic Accounting Theory*. The following extracts from this report (slightly amended in the interest of continuity) demonstrate the sort of approach that might be used in drafting a code; and they also provide some examples of nice accounting language.

> Accounting is the process of identifying, measuring, and communicating economic information to permit informed judgments and decisions by users of the information. . . . Economics is concerned with any situation in which a choice must be made involving scarce resources. . . . The all-inclusive criterion is the usefulness of the information. . . . The objectives of accounting are to provide information for the following purposes:
>
> 1) Making decisions concerning the use of limited resources.
> 2) Effectively directing and controlling an organization's human and material resources.
> 3) Maintaining and reporting on the custodianship of resources.
> 4) Facilitating social functions and controls.
>
> In the area of internal management—administrative direction and control—accounting information is used to facilitate the formulation and execution of plans. Through systematic record-keeping, special investigations, and analyses of data, accounting makes possible efficiency in the acquisition, maintenance, and use of the resources required by the plans. Accounting also plays a role in the motivation of individuals and groups charged with developing and carrying out plans, and it provides the major means of appraising the effectiveness with which individuals and groups perform their assignments.
>
> Other social functions in which accounting plays important roles include taxation, the prevention of fraud in a variety of contexts, governmental regulation of utilities, the activities of government in the general regulation and stimulation of commerce, management-labour relations, and the preparation of statistics on economic activity for the use of all interested persons. The accounting objective in this area is to facilitate the operations of organized society for the welfare of all.

The purpose of developing a theory of accounting is to establish standards for judging the acceptability of accounting methods. Procedures that meet the standards should be employed in the practice of accounting; those failing to meet the standards should be rejected.

The committee lays down the important standards for accounting, and it recommends that these should be: (1) relevance; (2) verifiability; (3) freedom from bias; and (4) quantifiability. In the committee's opinion, relevance is the basic consideration—and this is very much my own view. In fact, without relevance, none of the other standards really matters.

Important Considerations

I suggest that a code of ground rules might be drafted along somewhat the following lines. Here, no attempt has been made to suggest appropriate language. I have attempted only to indicate the type of ideas that should be incorporated:

1) The sole purpose of financial statements is to provide useful information to those who need to be informed in order to carry out intelligently some economic activity.

2) The purpose of publishing financial statements of commercial enterprises is to show, for a given date, the strength of the enterprise and its earning power. What is required is a statement of assets and liabilities at this given date, and operating statements to indicate earning trends in the past (as a basis for estimating future earnings).

3) With regard to assets, the statement should show relative liquidity by distinguishing between current assets, which are available to meet current liabilities, and assets which will not normally be liquidated in the near future.

4) Assets must be stated in terms which measure their current value, because to determine overall trends in a company, it is essential to reach a meaningful figure for the total dollar value of the assets. Different kinds of assets must be converted to a relevant dollar equivalent. In reaching a satisfactory figure for current value, various procedures are useful—for example, values based on earning power, on appraisal, on replacement value, or on up-to-date market price.

In each case, it is a matter of judgment as to which procedure should be used in valuing an asset. The important principle is that procedures should be consistently applied in valuing a given type of asset, unless there is some reason to change procedures—in which case it is important that the change in procedure be disclosed whenever it has a material effect.

The problems involved in reaching a satisfactory current value will often be difficult; but they must be overcome. Anyone who purchases a property other than relatively standard merchandise faces the necessity of deciding what this property is worth in dollar equivalent. Without first determining this equivalent, he could not proceed with the purchase. This problem is also faced by anyone who invests in the shares of a company. He too must somehow determine the value of the company—from an earning-power or net-asset point of view, whichever seems most appropriate to him. In producing periodic financial statements, the accountant is simply aiding such an investor as best he can. With general purpose statements, the accountant does a similar service for the shareholder who is contemplating a sale of his shares, for creditors of the corporation, and for others who are interested in its financial strength.

5) Liabilities should be set forth in a classification which indicates the imminence of settlement. A financial statement should show when the liabilities become due.

It is important to avoid a legalistic view of liabilities. Any legal obligation of the company should of course be included; but it is also important to include liabilities which the company must meet even if these are not legally exigible at the balance-sheet date.

As assets are stated at their current value, it is only logical that liabilities should be stated at current value too. This step would involve an important and highly contentious departure from current accounting conventions. It would mean that long-term liabilities should be discounted to present value. This idea has often been dismissed as impractical; but with computerization, many difficult calculating problems which were previously too complicated to attempt can now be tackled. It should be remembered that the discounting of future liabilities would only be justified where material amounts were involved, and this would normally restrict the problem area to a relatively few long-term balance-sheet items. To be consistent, the current-value principle should be applied on the liability side of the balance sheet as well as on the asset side. I personally doubt that this is as outrageous a proposal as some people think it to be. In any event, the possibility should certainly be investigated.

6) An essential point to emphasize is that the financial statements issued by a commercial enterprise are *period* statements. They purport to show what happens from year to year, from month to month, or from quarter to quarter. To do this, they must be based on current values and each period must stand on its own feet.

7) The change in net assets indicates how the owner's equity in the company has increased (or decreased) during a given period. The operating statement of a commercial enterprise establishes the change in net assets by analysing the income and outgo for this period. For a meaningful figure of net income to be produced, the change in net assets must be analyzed into at least the following elements: (a) contributions or withdrawals by the owners; (b) operating income and outgo during the period (distinguishing between ordinary and extraordinary items); (c) holding gains and losses; and (d) adjustments of prior-year income.

8) It is my opinion that a satisfactory code can be produced only if we restrict our attention to commercial enterprises. (In this, I disagree with the report of the American Accounting Association Committee, from which I have quoted above. This report suggests that the same principles should apply to non-commercial organizations. But to my mind, a separate set of principles will be required for these; and I have several comments to make on this point in the next chapter.)

World of Change

Before leaving the question of an accounting code, one further point must be stressed. The term "code" suggests an elaborate statement which settles contentious matters with finality; in it, the great truths are set down in precise and careful terms. Thus, a code is, by nature, static.

We must remember, however, that we live in an age where change is the order of the day, and where developments come over the plate with bewildering rapidity. Under such circumstances, no code (no matter how well drawn) can expect to stay set for very long. Even if we succeeded in developing an ideal code (and of course we never will), we would have to keep changing it as conditions themselves changed.

In reform, the new ideas will presumably arise from new problems which come up on the firing line of actual practice. Practising accountants, with the assistance of the academic professionals, will have to find new solutions as new problems arise and as new techniques make better procedures available. It is to be hoped that the keepers of our accounting code (and I see this as the main responsibility of our professional institutes) will then select those developments which are of value and incorporate them into our code—thus keeping it up to date.

CHAPTER 7

Special Cases

One of the problems which has vexed the accounting profession in its seemingly endless search for a satisfactory statement of generally accepted accounting principles is the fact that the type of financial statements to which these principles should apply has not been clearly recognized and defined. We have become so accustomed to the conventional balance sheet and related income statement that we tend to forget that there are other types of accounting statements, and that special types of operation may require statements which are quite different from those which we have been talking about.

Profit may be determined, quite legitimately, in a number of different ways—depending on the purpose for which the profit figure is needed. The fact that profit can be determined in different ways creates no problem so long as those who are trying to interpret a statement understand the basis on which it has been prepared. In statements prepared for management, for example, different concepts may be introduced— because management, being in charge of the preparation of the statements, is in a position to appreciate the methods that have been used. It is not until we attempt to prepare statements which are intended to be useful to strangers or outsiders (i.e., people who are not "in the know") that we are obliged to find an agreed basis on which to prepare the statements. Thus, it is only when outsiders come to be considered that there is any necessity for a code of generally agreed-upon ground rules.

This point is of great importance; and failure to appreciate its significance leads to many arguments at cross-purposes. One such argument occurs when someone with management responsibility wishes to have a statement prepared for his own use on a particular basis—only to encounter the opposition of his accountant, who objects to the idea on the grounds that it is contrary to generally accepted accounting principles. It is only when a statement is intended for general use (that is to say, when it will be used by outsiders who have no special knowledge of the basis on which it is prepared) that there is any need to adhere to conventional rules of presentation. So long as the statement is being prepared for the manager's personal use, he is entitled to have it prepared on whatever principles he wishes.

To clarify and stress this point, it is necessary to refer briefly to various special areas where generally accepted accounting principles do not apply. The danger is that if we do not, then when we turn to consider what should be included in a code of ground rules, matters may be complicated by the inclusion of rules that are appropriate to specialized types of accounting to which the code itself should have no application. Thus, in this chapter, we shall consider several accounting areas in which general principles have no application.

Management Accounting

The managers of a business require statements for all sorts of purposes. For one thing, they need some kind of composite, overall picture of the total operations of the company for a given period of time—monthly, quarterly, or annually. Management's requirements in this respect are much the same as those of outsiders—shareholders, creditors, suppliers, and so on. General purpose statements give the best available picture of overall performance, and are thus of importance to management for comparison with the progress of competitors as disclosed in *their* published statements.

The published statements prepared for shareholders and others are therefore of some use to management, since they provide a general view of operations on the same basic principles that are used in other companies. Statements based on any other principles would lack comparability with other statements, and this would mean a serious loss of usefulness. Management often requires statements which contain more detail than would be appropriate for shareholders—but statements, nevertheless, which have been prepared on basically the same valuation principles.

When we turn our attention from overall statements to statements which are prepared for special purposes, we find that these latter statements need not be prepared on any prescribed basis. Special statements are intended to explore such questions as whether or not a certain product is profitable, whether a certain machine should be replaced, whether a new line should be taken on, whether an asset should be abandoned—and so on. Thus, the only thing that matters is that these statements provide the information which a manager needs. Various costing systems, such as direct costing or incremental costing, may be properly used—so long as they provide the specific data required. It is only when statements are produced to circulate generally (to become, as it were, "negotiable") that agreed principles have any propriety.

To illustrate this point, let us consider the calculation of net profit. For some purposes, it may be perfectly proper to calculate profit without, say, considering depreciation. However, it would be entirely wrong to publish a set of annual statements which describe a figure as net profit when that figure has been calculated without providing for depreciation —unless it is clearly disclosed that depreciation has not been provided for. Anyone who looks at a published income statement is entitled to assume that the net profit reported has been calculated after depreciation—unless the contrary is specifically stated.

Taxable Income

Income tax has become one of the most important facts of life in our economy. With corporation tax rates commonly around the 50-percent level, the determination of taxable income on a fair basis becomes a high priority requirement. It is essential that all taxpayers be treated fairly; and this can only be assured if taxable income is determined on the same principles for each taxpayer, and if the principles are fair. The more closely taxable income corresponds to the real increase of wealth during the taxation period, the fairer the spreading of the tax burden will be. Thus, in determining taxable income, we arrive at the same goal as we agreed upon when considering net income for published accounting reports.

This same conclusion may be reached by yet another line of reasoning. Those responsible for tax administration must arrive at a figure of taxable income on a uniform basis for everyone. There are, theoretically, two ways of doing this. The Department of Taxation can accept net profit as calculated by the generally accepted accounting principles which apply to the formal published statements; or the department can work out its own way of calculating net profit. While these two theoretical possibilities exist, it is surely self-evident that in practice, the second method is out of the question. For the department to set out to draft its own principles of determining income would present it with an almost impossible task. And even if the department were able, somehow or other, to produce a set of principles, these would presumably be very similar to the generally accepted principles which we now use for formal financial statements. The reason for this is that the department would be trying to do just what the accounting profession is trying to do in drawing up its rules for the determination of profit—i.e., to find a figure which would represent increase in wealth during the period. It is not surprising, therefore, that tax departments have tended by and large to go along with generally accepted accounting principles—but with a few modifications. These modifications we should now consider.

If the department's only object were to collect tax fairly from everyone, there would be little reason to depart from generally accepted accounting principles. However, things are not that simple. All countries tend to use their tax system for purposes other than the equitable collection of revenue. Various kinds of incentives and deterrents get built into the system in the form of special reductions in tax to stimulate certain projects or certain depressed areas, or to encourage activities which the government thinks desirable—like oil exploration or research. Thus, considerations enter into the determination of taxable income which have no place in the determining of net profit for published statements.

Another complication arises from the fact that every time you report a dollar of income, fifty cents of it is snatched away by the government. When a taxpayer is required to assess himself (as our system requires him to do), and when every dollar he estimates that he earns adds to the tax he must pay, income determination takes on a special piquance.

Consider the difficult area of capital cost allowances—or depreciation, as it is popularly (but less accurately) called. Determining an appropriate rate of depreciation involves an estimate of the useful life of the asset, and this estimate has got to be rough and ready. Physical wear and tear can only be roughly forecast, and the prediction of obsolescence is truly an insoluble problem. New inventions and changes in style may play havoc with the most reasonable estimates of useful life.

Amidst these vagaries, tax departments have found it necessary to establish arbitrary ceilings for depreciation rates in order to prevent too rapid an amortization of fixed assets, with a corresponding deferment of tax payment. The result is that tax departments tend to rely on generally accepted accounting principles, but introduce certain special provisions in some areas to remove from taxpayers the temptation to defer payments unreasonably—and thus to gain an unfair advantage over other taxpayers.

A recent Royal Commission in Canada examined the entire tax system of the country and came up with a mammoth report. After listening to representations from The Canadian Institute of Chartered Accountants, the commission decided not to recommend that taxable income be determined in accordance with generally accepted accounting principles. However, the chairman of the commission, Kenneth LeM. Carter, a chartered accountant, wrote what was in effect a brief dissent on this point. In doing so, he stated very clearly the relationship between taxable income and income determined on ordinary accounting principles. These are his words: "For its own particular purposes, tax legislation must continue to provide for departures from accepted accounting practices. But in my view, they should be as few as possible and all set forth in the taxing statutes. The most obvious of the departures is capital cost allowances."

The relationship between taxable income and net profit for purposes of financial statements should be clear. The tax department cannot be expected to accept, for tax purposes, methods of calculating income which are not generally accepted in financial reporting. Since it must treat all taxpayers alike, the tax department cannot be expected to produce new and better ways of determining income. However, if better ways are developed and are eventually accepted, the tax department can have no alternative but to follow on by accepting such changes as the correct method of determining taxable income.

When improvements in accounting are being debated (improvements, for example, such as substituting current value for cost), the matter should be decided on the basis of which figure leads to the best method of determining income for purposes of general reporting. If the new method gains acceptance for this purpose, it too must be eventually accepted in determining taxable income. But, until the new method is recognized as being generally accepted, the department has no alternative but to continue assessing on the old basis.

Non-Commercial Enterprises

Interesting sidelights are cast on the problems of accounting principles by a consideration of those enterprises which are not organized for profit.

There are a great variety of undertakings that come under this general heading. Some of them require financial statements in virtually the same form as those which are designed for commercial enterprises; others have quite different problems and are best treated differently. In establishing rules for the production of financial statements for commercial enterprises, the question that inevitably dominates our thinking is the question of a realistic determination of net profit for the period. But when we turn to an enterprise which is *not* concerned with profit-making, it is almost inconceivable that the rules thus developed will be completely appropriate.

For charitable corporations, government departments, hospitals, universities, and many other types of operation, the earning of net income is not a primary objective. Such enterprises really require special investigation. However, there has been very little consideration of their problems; and unfortunately, the notion has got about that it is desirable for all such organizations to run on what is described as "business-like" lines. It thus tends to become almost a point of honour for such institutions to produce something that resembles, as closely as possible, the balance sheet and income statement of a corporation. These statements dutifully report something described as "excess of expenditure over income," which, insofar as it has any meaning, is a misleading term. Sometimes the exigencies of the figures make it inevitable that the statements show an excess of income over expenditure. And this is worse than misleading. It is, in fact, calamitous—since a charitable institution is in danger of losing all support if it appears to be prosperous.

Many of these institutions are, in effect, acting in a position of trust —for example, charitable institutions which receive donations and pay them out for welfare purposes, or executors who receive money for the beneficiaries of an estate and pay it out to them. In such cases, there is no question of earnings or profitability. There is simply the question of whether statutory or testamentary provisions have been carried out properly. The statements in such cases should be designed specifically to demonstrate whether or not this is the case.

The important point for us to grasp is that the principles of commercial accounting do not necessarily apply. I believe that a different type of accounting should be developed for non-profit bodies—but such an undertaking lies beyond the scope of this book.

Special Cases of Commercial Enterprises

The generally accepted rules, no matter how well conceived, will not even be suitable for all types of profit-making enterprise. It is perhaps worth examining an instance of this type of unsuitability for the light that it throws on the nature of our accounting code. For this purpose, mutual life insurance companies provide an interesting case in point.

It has already been explained that the key to the statements of an ordinary commercial enterprise is that they are designed to set forth the financial strength of the company and the important trends in its operations. Thus, the balance sheet is a document of basic significance, since it shows the net assets of the company at a given date. This establishes the shareholders' equity, and each shareholder can then calculate his share of that equity by simply comparing the number of shares he owns to the total shares outstanding. Similarly, he can easily estimate his share of net income earned.

In the case of a mutual life insurance company, the balance sheet is, relatively speaking, a much less informative document. A very similar looking sort of balance sheet can, of course, be produced—the assets being offset against liabilities, reserves, and surplus. So far so good. But the policyholder, who is the owner of the business (just as the shareholder would be were it not a mutual company), cannot make a simple calculation to determine his share of the surplus. The share of the surplus that is attributable to a policyholder depends on the type of policy he holds, the experience of the company in that class of insurance, the length of time the policy has been in force, and so on. Consequently, there is no way of determining from the balance sheet of a mutual life insurance company what part of the equity is properly attributable to different individuals. The equity of the policyholder can only be established by a quite elaborate actuarial calculation.

Life insurance companies have often been a target of criticism for the fact that their conventional financial statements are not more informative. The fact remains that the conventional balance sheet and income statement are inevitably much less informative for this class of company because of the nature of their business. What progressive companies do in order to overcome this difficulty is not to try to produce better balance sheets, but to publish a good deal of statistical information about business-in-force, new business written, mortality experience, and so on. By considering such statistics, the policyholder can inform himself on the strength and progress of the company. And it is this kind of information which a shareholder or creditor should get from the financial statements of a merchandising or manufacturing enterprise.

The case of mutual life insurance companies has been mentioned because it throws further light on the essential limitations in the applicability of generally accepted accounting rules. We would think much more clearly about accounting principles if we were to keep these essential limitations in mind. Many other examples could be cited of special types of operation which require their own code of rules.

*   *   *

This brief review of some of the areas to which generally accepted ground rules would not apply is intended only to mark some limits on the task before us. In subsequent chapters, we undertake to consider only those rules which should apply to the published financial statements of the general run of commercial enterprises.

CHAPTER 8

Prerequisites for Progress

We now approach the halfway stage in this dissertation. So far, I have tried to explain why we must have better statements and have indicated the theoretical basis on which they could be produced. However, even if the theoretical case for current values has been convincingly made, I have no expectation that better statements will actually be published if the matter is left at this point. From Chapter 9 onwards, therefore, I shall deal with the manner in which improvements could actually be put into effect in order to achieve the kind of statement which I have argued we should have. Before embarking on a discussion of the problems of implementation, however, I should like in this chapter to review very briefly the main thread of the argument and to comment on certain other questions.

An Interim Review

At the expense of even greater repetition than I have already been guilty of, let me just say that I have attempted to demonstrate that we can produce better statements only if we accept current value as the primary and basic objective in accounting.

I have explained where we got off the track. It was sensible at first to develop accounting rules from an analysis of accounting practices, meeting difficulties as they arose. Starting with simple records of receipts and disbursements (according to my completely unresearched view of accounting history), we developed accrual techniques and the depreciation concepts which answered well enough the practical problems which we at first encountered. In the process, we reached a form of statement which, in spite of a certain amount of routine grumbling, was so generally accepted that proposals for reform raised little enthusiasm. The trouble was that while we appeared to be progressing satisfactorily, we were in fact rolling, not down a broad highway, but up a blind alley. By this process, we have finally reached a point at which no further progress can be made (at least, no progress of any importance) until we retrace our steps and start out on another track.

The end of a blind alley is a particularly uncomfortable spot when one's world is in the midst of hectic changes. In the world of accounting, new requirements are arising continuously, and the accounting profession must be on its toes, ready to make the startling advances that will be necessary if we are to keep up with the demands for our services. The only direction to sprint when you are in a blind alley is back down the alley—in the hope you can get back onto the main road.

We need not only to *keep* up with developments, we need also to *catch* up with them. This is illustrated in the rapid expansion of worldwide trade and investment. In spite of rising nationalism and the passing of the old colonial trading systems, merchandise is traded across international boundaries more freely than ever; and international investments are rising rapidly. Thus, companies that are establishing plants in foreign countries already need better accounting facilities to manage the more complicated operations which result. The trouble is that we are scarcely in a position to provide such services. We must catch up with these demands and gird our loins to meet future requirements which are almost certain to be still more exacting—and we will never succeed in doing this unless our financial reports are logically based.

Objections—Real and Phoney

There will be no improvement in financial reporting unless leaders in the business world become convinced that changes should be made. By definition, a leader is someone who has done all right under the present ground rules. And having learned to cope with these rules, he is almost certain to prefer the present system to some new proposal—even if the proposal sounds like a sensible development. Naturally, no one talks as though this were the case. A business leader is hardly likely to say: "Look here, old boy, what you recommend sounds like a great idea. But I personally am doing all right, and I do not relish, at my age and eminence, the idea of starting all over again trying to learn new tricks." Instead, the leader attempts to rationalize his position.

There is not much room in which to defend our present system in theoretical argument. The usual rationalization of the *status quo* is on the practical grounds that the valuation processes inherent in current-value accounting would be unreliable and not sufficiently objective. The answer to objections about the reliability of valuation procedures is easy. Some processes are as reliable and as objective as historical cost—for example, quoted market prices for securities or commodities. Other processes, although open to abuse, are nevertheless permitted in conventional accounting. Take the question of appraisals for land, buildings, and machinery. In Canada and the United States, while such appraisals are not normally encouraged in the best circles, they are sanctioned in some cases—as, for example, when reorganizations or quasi-reorganizations or mergers have taken place. Moreover, in both countries, valuations are accepted in cases where inventory is written down. And it should be remembered that while this involves a write-down of the current period's income, it means an automatic write-up of the following period's income. Current-value accounting would simply extend the use of appraisal techniques that are already countenanced. And it is hard to believe that the systematic use of such techniques could be more objectionable than the haphazard use which is now sanctioned.

To argue that we should insist on a cost base because it is more reliable, would be about as logical as saying to someone who wants to know the way to the Grand Canyon: "I am not too sure about that, so I will explain precisely how to get to New York City because I happen to have a map of that area." Would it not be more helpful to say "The Grand Canyon is about a thousand miles west of here," even if it turned out that the Grand Canyon was actually more like 800 miles away and the direction was actually west-northwest-by-west? The precise way to New York City is presumably of no interest to the inquirer; while the information about the Grand Canyon, although not accurate and not supported by producible data, does at least suggest that it is too far to drive in a day but could probably be driven in two days, that it would probably take an hour or two to fly there, and so on. Carrying this illustration a step further, if the inquiry had been about the way to Jersey City, a reply such as "I do not know, but here is the way to New York City" would make sense because the two places are close together. In the same way, cost is likely to be useful information when it approximates current value—and not otherwise.

It is perhaps worth emphasizing that the real trouble with the cost basis is not that costs are necessarily out of date, but that a cost-based balance sheet states a given asset at a mélange of different cost levels. If, for example, a balance sheet which was issued in 1968 stated the fixed assets at 1950 price levels, the analyst could at least discover the price-level change for the intervening period and thus bring the fixed-asset cost more or less up to date. But this is not the situation. When a 1968 balance sheet presents fixed assets at cost, such cost is a mixture of price levels. Most of the assets may have been purchased recently, and the cost figure may be of considerable significance—or, on the other hand, most of the assets may have been purchased long ago at entirely different price levels. The statement-user simply doesn't know which is the case, and he therefore has no way of making sensible calculations. This is why it is so important for the accountant to do the estimating of values when he prepares the statements—since only he is in a position to make them knowledgeably.

Finally, while a switch to current values would undoubtedly introduce a larger element of subjective judgment, the choice is not between a completely objective system and a highly subjective one. It has already been pointed out that some current values may be objectively determined, and the converse is equally true—that is, that under our present rules some of the "objectivity" is a bit thin. For example, how reliable is the cost of an article as an "objective" valuation when someone pays twice too much for it? And how far does the accountant probe to see if this is the case when he gets an authentic receipted invoice presented to him?

The Distribution of Food, Both Intellectual and Physical

Accountants are distributors of intellectual nourishment, and I sometimes think that we could learn a good deal from the food distribution industry. In food marketing, many problems are encountered which parallel those which we meet in distributing financial data. Food may be contaminated; it may bear misleading labels; a dishonest grocer may overcharge for it, or he may misrepresent its qualities—in short, all sorts of terrible things can happen to it. And in a way, this is all quite similar to the fraudulent and misleading information that can be distributed in the business world —while all the while the need for good information is urgent.

Nevertheless, in spite of the range of possible abuses, the regular distribution of wholesome food is an essential function in our society. If the food industry had devoted itself wholeheartedly to the prevention of abuses, we would never have had the wonderfully easy and efficient food-marketing system which we have become so accustomed to on this continent. And yet, the dangers of bad food have not been ignored. After all, we do have pure food laws, labelling regulations, sanitary inspection, and other precautions.

In accounting, on the other hand, I sometimes feel that we have devoted almost our entire thought and energy to devising ways of preventing the circulation of misleading data. It is true that precautions of this sort are necessary; at the same time, I do think that we have overdone them. It is now time to divert some of our attention to facilitating the exchange of financial data between people who want to communicate honestly.

In this connection, it is a great pity that some of the tentative efforts to introduce useful price-level data into statements have been attacked on the grounds that to permit this sort of thing might open the way to abuse. If honestly used, this practice would also open the way to more informative statements. The "bad guys" are a small minority, and surely we can devise ways of coping with them without discouraging the exchange of useful information.

The Academics

Some consideration should now be given to the position of the academic wing of the profession. As might be expected, the academics produce most of the quality writing on accounting theory that fills our technical journals. Since they tend to be intellectually lively (relatively speaking) and individualistic, they naturally present many different kinds of opinions. However, I believe that a substantial majority of professors accept the logic of some kind of current-value accounting. For example, many articles have appeared in journals such as *The Accounting Review* pointing out the desirability and feasibility of adopting current values. And to my mind, these arguments are irrefutable.

My quarrel with the academics does not concern the question of what our objective should be: it concerns, instead, the manner in which they interpret the accounting process. From their writings, I get the feeling that some of them inhabit a never-never land in which an attempt is made to extrapolate a fairly simple and straightforward set of ground rules into a profound philosophic system—a system based on eternal verities and bedrock postulates of self-evident efficacy.

As I have said before, accounting is a purely utilitarian craft—and it does not bother me that this is so. Florence Nightingale founded the modern nursing profession on a few elementary maxims of hygiene which she developed in the fetid air of a Crimean military hospital. And is not the whole prestigious medical profession based on the wholly utilitarian project of healing the sick? Yet, in much academic writing, we get the impression that there should be something more to accounting than just pragmatic rules. For the life of me, I do not understand what is wrong with pragmatism. To what higher function can an accountant aspire than to develop the art of financial communication?

There are all sorts of intellectual difficulties to cope with in accounting: questions of the application of mathematics to the measurement of assets, questions of sociological and psychological approaches to decision-making, questions of data-processing techniques in an electronic age, questions of projecting future probabilities, and so on. Obviously, there is an eminently respectable academic content to the discipline. But this does not mean, so far as I can see, that we need an elaborate philosophic analysis in order to determine the basic objectives of the art—particularly when these objectives are crystal clear and unmistakable in the light of ordinary common sense.

I have remarked on other occasions that I have great admiration for products of accounting research such as *AICPA Research Studies*, Numbers 1 and 3. I believe that these studies reach basically sound conclusions. But at the same time, I can't help feeling that such conclusions are clouded to some extent by irrelevant philosophic digressions which militate against acceptance.

Deductive and Inductive Reasoning

My criticism of the approach of some academic confrères gets down to arguments about the superiority of conclusions reached by deductive reasoning. As I understand it, the formulation of "principles" from an observation of actual transactions (an inductive process) is somehow felt to be intrinsically inferior to the process of discovering basic postulates and deriving principles by logical argument from such postulates. We hear such remarks as: "Accounting must be something more than a mere distillation from practice." In response, I ask: "Why?" Both deductive and inductive approaches are legitimate, and each has its appropriate applications. In fact, in many cases, the two methods are used in harness —general hypotheses being checked by the collection of observed data, and new theories then being induced from such observations—a process which one could imagine reciprocating indefinitely. This is presumably what the great Swedish economist, Gustav Cassel, was trying to say when he wrote:

> I did not begin my scientific work by conceiving a ready-made system from which every truth could be deduced and into which the reality had at any price to be pressed in order to fit. This is no truly scientific way of going to work. If, as I think, my different investigations form a unity

which in some sense can be called an economic system, although by no means complete, it is because I have tried at every step to let my aims and methods be determined solely by the essential *economic* nature of the subject to be investigated. If we consistently observe this rule I think we should find that, in economic theory, there is not so much room for arbitrary decisions as has generally been believed. In fact, there is much of necessity in economic life and also much of necessity in the ways of analysing this life. The important thing is just to find out these necessities. If we try to do this, and if we keep our attention constantly directed upon what is, from a purely economic point of view, essentially the matter we have to investigate, our results will prove to possess a natural coherency and logical unity.[11]

I cannot believe that a modern Descartes ("I spend, therefore I am") would get very far in trying to build up a system of financial communications by searching his inner consciousness—no matter how diligently he searched. To build such a system, he would have to get right into the midst of commercial life, observing and seeing what is required. In short, accounting ground rules *must* be a distillation from practice.

I have always felt that the English and history departments of universities provide a better model for business schools than do the science departments. There can be valid intellectual approaches other than the scientific approach, and we gain little by trying to mould what is essentially an art into a scientific discipline.

Our professors have a lot of important work to do in shaping accounting theory; but they must, like the rest of us, get off on the right foot by frankly recognizing usefulness as the sole and sufficient aim in financial reporting.

Research

It is, of course, very difficult to assess the quantity and quality of basic accounting research that is being carried out at our universities. It is true that some impressive articles appear in our professional journals. Nevertheless, it is hard to detect any practical application of the results of basic research to the production of statements. Without in any way sitting in judgment on the basic research of academics, it seems safe to say that for the accountant-in-practice and the accountant-in-industry (both of whom are responsible for statement production), the term "research" has tended to be used to describe a process which has gone something like this:

1) Some association of accountants, disturbed about critical comments from the public, sets up a committee to "do something about it."

11. Gustav Cassel, *Fundamental Thoughts in Economics*. T. Fisher Unwin, London, 1925.

Often (perhaps typically) the committee is made up of a good cross-section of the association's livelier members.

2) By corresponding with one another, and by discussion, the members of the committee come to agreement on what they consider to be the most frequent and important complaints. These they sort out into some scheme of priority—and thus, a "research" program is established.

3) Taking the selected topics one by one, the committee then debates them and finally issues some sort of pronouncement on each in turn.

I have been involved in as much of this sort of thing as the next man, and I have found it stimulating, educational, and "worthwhile." Moreover, I am not in the least ashamed of the results. Accounting "bulletins" have stirred up much discussion (a good thing in itself) and have probably been responsible for most of the progress that has been made in financial reporting over the past twenty-five years or so. As a profession, we should view our accomplishments in this area with pride; they are admirable and praiseworthy. The only trouble is that they are totally inadequate in the crisis in which we happen to find ourselves at the present moment. We have been caught up in the computer age, and the steady respectable progress that we have been making cannot possibly do the job which we must do if we are to survive as a profession.

Our research committees have been composed of extremely busy people. (No one seems to take much interest in the opinions of someone who is not busy.) They have therefore had to rely on two techniques: (1) meetings at which committee members hammer out a joint statement (often through a dozen laborious drafts); and (2) projects assigned to individual members of the profession (usually academics) in which they prepare "research papers" on specific problem areas. Of the research papers, some have been extremely good. But anyone who has been set up with a budget to study a congenial topic can be expected to produce something challenging and stimulating and highly individualistic. Moreover, it would be very difficult to demonstrate that such papers had, in fact, led to much improvement of the end product in the accounting process—i.e., financial statements. As to the group discussions, these have almost necessarily proceeded by declamation: "In my opinion, the straight-line method tends to produce the most reliable results." "I can't agree with you, the sum of digit method has the advantage of. . . ." "Why worry so much about depreciation when what's really wrong, in my opinion, is a failure to adopt LIFO more generally." "Well, that's all very well, but SEC would never stand for it." And so on.

This is all very well. But it simply is not good enough in a computerized age. What we must do is to link up more effectively our basic research efforts with the hammering out of our code of practical ground rules and our evolving accounting procedures. Let us illustrate this crucial point with an example.

One of the key objections to the acceptance of current values is that the resulting asset values would be too subjective—that is, that they would depend too much on the individual whim or predilection of the accountant who happens to be preparing the statement. This is clearly a legitimate thing to worry about. But how serious is the danger? I can just imagine how the point would have been explored by some of the accounting committees on which I have served. It would have been argued on a *Yes it would - No it wouldn't* basis, with everyone putting his oar in. The resulting decision (if ever one were reached) would tend to be some sort of elaborate compromise. Proceeding, thus, by declamation and pontification is of no use whatever. What we need is a clear answer which is factually supported by actual research into the question. If we are to expect a new approach (such as current-value accounting) to gain acceptance, then we must be able to state to what extent the danger of subjective judgments is likely to be detrimental. And we must be able to support our contention with something more solid than "what we think will happen."

This opens up tremendous possibilities for effective research—i.e., research that is firmly tied to the ultimate decision-making on large issues. In *The Journal of Accounting Research* (Spring 1968), there is a beautiful example of the approach that is required—a project by Professor Daniel L. McDonald in which he sought to explore the degree of subjectivity that might be introduced by adopting the current-value concept. The results are written up in the journal and are well worth studying. In this project, it was assumed that in worrying about valuations which are too subjective, one of the things we fear is widely differing valuations depending on the individual who prepares the statement. Thus, two groups of twenty accountants were given the particulars of a fleet of motor cars. Those in one group were asked to value the fleet on the basis of generally accepted accounting principles, and those in the other group to value the fleet on net realizable value. Analysing the results, Professor McDonald concluded that there was a significantly wider range of valuations in the group which had used generally accepted accounting principles.

Admittedly, a single experiment of this sort is not conclusive. But surely it is a step in the right direction. Since the criterion of dispersal is not the only way to test for subjectivity, let us then develop other tests. The groups were small, so let us try the experiment with larger groups. Motor cars present a problem that is quite different from other kinds of asset—for example, land or buildings. Hence, let us see what would result from a test of these other assets. With our highly developed business schools at the university level, and with the enormous outpouring of financial statements of all kinds, we have inexhaustible facilities for research. Clearly, we must start basing our pronouncements on actual study and not on simple pontification.

The Need For Venturesomeness

It is my belief that those who have the responsibility for issuing financial statements must take the initiative if we are ever to see any improvement. Unless they are determined to do their part, very little can be accomplished. I therefore devote the remaining chapters of this book to a detailed consideration of the ways in which better statements could be issued right now—without benefit of any official pronouncements or meetings of professional accounting committees. I try to demonstrate that for those who are bold enough, radically better presentations are immediately possible; and for those who are cautious and would prefer to start gently, smaller steps can be taken to effect more moderate improvements.

Motivation

While I believe that improvements can be quite readily introduced, obviously nothing will happen unless those who issue statements genuinely want to describe more clearly what is actually going on. There must be a real desire to communicate—and this is a tougher problem than it may at first appear.

It can be argued that the less information that management give out, the less likely they are to find themselves second-guessed and interfered with. And in view of the great pressures which are inevitably part of running a large corporation, it is understandable that management's most cherished wish might be to be left alone, undisturbed, to grapple with their troubles. However, the tide is running strongly in the direction of more disclosure. Thus, whether they like it or not, management is bound to be more and more under scrutiny. If they can look beyond their immediate troubles, it should be possible to conclude that in the

long run the more realistic accounting reports are, the better the
economy will run. In other words, if a broad view is taken, anyone who
believes in free enterprise should insist on the best communication
system that can be devised.

Other Contributions

While the chief onus for initiating improvements is, as I have said, on
management, there are others who also have serious parts to play. The
academic accountants, quite apart from the responsibility of turning out
good accountants, have before them all sorts of fields which cry out for
research. Marvin L. Stone provides this authoritative summing up of the
situation:

> Once you are convinced of the need for research, you need not look
> very far for subjects which need investigation. The problem is mainly
> one of assigning priorities. Naturally, each of us would put potential
> projects in a different order. Academicians probably favor basic re-
> search; practitioners probably seek the practical answers to immediate
> problems which might be provided by applied research. But there is
> really no reason to argue about what ought to be done first. So much
> needs doing, it is just a question of determining how to get on with the
> job as expeditiously and efficiently as possible. Substantial strides have
> been taken in the last few years, but they really have not made much
> of a dent in the pile. So far, the efforts have mainly succeeded in
> whetting our appetites for all that could be done. Research, by its very
> nature, begets more research, because increased knowledge makes us
> aware of how ignorant we are.[12]

The practising professional accountants, with their institutes, have a
primary responsibility for developing a genuinely useful code of accounting principles—although accountants in teaching and in management
also have important parts to play in this undertaking. The practising
accountants, moreover, also have a major role to play, as consultants and
auditors, in aiding and encouraging the publication of better reports.

Government regulatory agencies can, of course, play a key role in
clearing the way for new experiments and in encouraging them. Since
these agencies spend most of their time watching for the bad guys, they
are not likely to think in terms of encouraging new schemes. But they
must remember that it is even more important to encourage full communication between honest people than it is to discourage the deceptions
of a sinister minority.

In informal rulings during the severe devaluation of sterling in

12. Marvin L. Stone, "Problems in Search of Solutions Through Research," *Empirical Re-*
search in Accounting: Selected Studies, 1968.

1967, the Securities and Exchange Commission encouraged companies under its jurisdiction to defer to future years any profit which they had made on such devaluation—but provided, at the same time, that any loss should be immediately taken up. Such actions are said to be "conservative." But how can we hope to get proper accounting if we do not abandon the mode of thought which motivates such actions? It is most important to consider the results that flow from this sort of "conservative" thinking—particularly in view of the fact that it represents the general attitude of security regulating agencies and others who seek, with admirable intentions, responsible financial presentation.

In a situation such as that which resulted in the 1967 ruling, there are three possible cases to consider. First, if a corporation did not have an important position in sterling (debit or credit) when devaluation occurred, it would not matter what sort of accounting it used. Secondly, if a company had a significant excess of sterling assets over liabilities, it would suffer a significant loss as the result of devaluation. Everyone agrees that the loss should be taken up—so that's fine. There remains the third case of the corporation which has a significant net liability in sterling. Such a corporation would make an exchange profit. Current-value accounting would require that the entire profit be taken up as of the devaluation date, whereas the "conservative" option would spread the profit over several years. Let us follow this case through and see where the sensible course lies.

Suppose that a corporation realized a $200,000 profit on the 1967 devaluation of sterling, and consider how its reported earnings would compare if the profit was taken up immediately—as compared with taking up the profit over a period of, say, five years:

Year	Profit disregarding exchange gain	Profit if exchange gain is taken up	
		(a) at once	(b) over 5 years
1965	$175,000	$175,000	$175,000
1966	150,000	150,000	150,000
1967	140,000	340,000	180,000
1968	160,000	160,000	200,000
1969	170,000	170,000	210,000
1970	190,000	190,000	230,000

The 5-year column gives a nice bland picture. But is that what we want? Admittedly, under current-value accounting, which is represented in column (a) above, the earnings for 1967 take some explaining. However, the exchange gain would be disclosed, and although it dwarfs the operating profits, it is nonetheless a genuine gain of the period. With the 5-year deferral, shown in column (b), think of all the continuing confusion. There is the exchange gain to explain in 1967 (just as there would be under current-value accounting), and the same problem persists for another four years. Moreover, in each of these four subsequent years, the corporation takes in an exchange profit which it did not earn in such years. For example, when the 1968 profits are published, the corporation would presumably report to its shareholders along the following lines: "Profits for the year were $200,000, including $40,000 arising from the 1967 devaluation of sterling. Shareholders may be pleased to note that this is the first time our profits have reached the $200,000 level." Something of this sort is accurate enough. But what will the newspaper headlines be? Perhaps:

RECORD YEAR

FOR X CO.

Profits at All-Time High

Well, the profits are not at an all-time high on any reasonable basis of calculation. And isn't anyone interested in logic any more? When, through the exigencies of the market place, we get so little opportunity to be logical, why should we go out of our way to demand a treatment for exchange profits that is different from our treatment for losses?

The classical subterfuge, sought by those who defend this kind of thing, is to stress the risk inherent in the fact that the exchange gain may be only temporary. But if we recorded only developments which we were certain were going to prove permanent, we would produce some pretty weird statements. I wish sterling well, with all my heart. But is there anyone who thinks that the likelihood of sterling's rising against the dollar is so great that we should require corporations who made a gain in the 1967 devaluation to keep some of that gain available to offset subsequent losses? Again, suppose that the corporation has subsequently liquidated its sterling holdings and would now be unaffected by a sterling recovery. Or suppose that it had become much more deeply committed in sterling. There are, in fact, many possible developments. But it would be difficult to conceive of one of them which would justify deferring the realized exchange gain.

Machiavelli has pointed out that there is nothing more difficult or more unsure of results than to take the lead in establishing a new order of things. Had he known the modern accounting profession, he might have put the matter more strongly still. It is a chilling reflection that, with the exception of the academics, all of the groups mentioned (management, accounting profession, and government regulators) are profoundly caution-oriented, and are about as attached to the *status quo* as anyone could be. It is for this reason that proposals which are, in effect, relatively moderate proposals require such impassioned urging.

CHAPTER 9

Essential First Steps

Up to this point, we have simply reviewed the current state of accounting theory and have proposed a better set of ground rules for the preparation of statements. There is nothing very new in the ideas that have so far been described. In such an exercise, there is always plenty of room for disagreement on specific points. The ground rules can be argued several ways, and when we get down to the details of accounting procedures there is all sorts of room for different opinions.

Up to now, the whole discussion has been intended to bring out one essential point—namely, that if better statements are to be produced, they must be statements which more closely approximate current values. Whether we recognize it or not, whether statement-users want it or not, whether the idea is familiar or unfamiliar—if the question is squarely faced, it must be conceded that in order to make sound economic decisions, it is desirable to have data that comes as close as possible to reflecting actual economic conditions. There can be doubt about the reliability of different valuation processes; but there can be no doubt that our ultimate objective is to produce statements which closely reflect the economic facts of life.

The Accounting Process

All that has been attempted so far is to establish a clear-cut goal towards which accounting reforms can be directed. It may take many years before accounting theory is developed to a really satisfactory state—and in fact, in a changing environment, the work of developing accounting theories must be continuous. However much we may perfect accounting theory, we shall not, in the process, necessarily produce better statements. This will only come if those who publish statements actually accept the challenge to produce better ones.

As the production of better financial statements is the main object of this text, we must, at this point, turn our attention from accounting theory and consider, from scratch, how we can actually move towards this goal of better published statements. I have already insisted that the direct responsibility for effecting improvements must rest on those who publish the statements—which means, of course, the managements of our commercial enterprises. The management of any enterprise is likely to be a rather complicated group. The boards of directors, the chief executive officer, the vice-president (finance), and various subsidiary officials—all these play a part in the production. It frequently happens that an effort on the part of some members of the management team to produce better statements is frustrated by the opposition of other members. If top management is not absolutely determined to produce better statements, then better statements will not be produced. We may remind ourselves of the point, alluded to previously, that management may have to take a long-term view if it is to work up any enthusiasm for better (and therefore more revealing) statements. In other words, management must believe that better reporting is, in itself, a good thing. When management produce statements, they must think less of what the immediate effect on their company's financial position will be if a certain disclosure is made, and more about whether or not fair reporting requires the disclosure. This may sound like a sort of scoutmaster's admonition, but we might as well stop pretending that we are going to produce more informative statements without genuinely seeking to communicate more fairly and frankly.

Before tackling the practical problems of statement production, we might do well to review the accounting process from the actual transactions of a corporation through to the ultimate decision by investors as to whether they should buy or sell its shares. It seems to me that this process involves five distinguishable stages and can be portrayed as shown in the chart on the following page. The five stages are the following:

STAGE A: RECORDING

As accounting is transaction-based, the first problem is to record accurately all transactions—receipts, disbursements, sales, purchases, and so on. These must be accurately recorded in a form which facilitates sum-

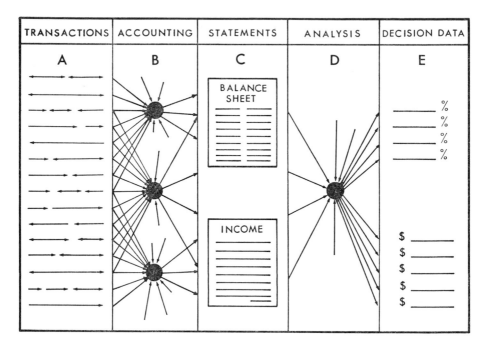

TRANSACTIONS	ACCOUNTING	STATEMENTS	ANALYSIS	DECISION DATA
A	B	C	D	E

From Raw Transactions to Usable Economic Data

marization into significant totals. There are interesting problems here of handling multitudinous data accurately and promptly, but this is not an important area for judgmental decisions. Good internal control is essential. Computers are more and more taking over this work. The independent auditor, while doing much less detailed checking than used to be thought desirable, still retains the responsibility for making certain that appropriate control systems are in effect.

STAGE B: ACCOUNTING ADJUSTMENTS

While accurately summarized transactions provide a base for statements, a number of non-transaction adjustments must be made by the management team in order to produce meaningful statements. It is at this stage that some of the matters which we have been discussing enter the picture. For example, it is here that the adjustments of assets and liabilities are decided upon, and it is at this point that good ground rules and good judgment have their effect.

The management team is responsible for making the non-transaction adjustments properly. The independent auditor's job is to review this work and to report whether or not, in his opinion, the statements produced by this process have been prepared on a basis which is consistent with that used in prior years and in conformity with generally accepted principles of accounting.

STAGE C: STATEMENTS

As the result of Stages A and B, financial statements emerge. These are officially the responsibility of the board of directors, and must therefore be finally approved by the board. The statements have been prepared by a complicated division of responsibility which runs, normally, from the accounting department up to the chief executive officer of the corporation through a vice-president in charge of finance. Independent auditors review the whole statement-production process, perform such tests as they consider in their professional judgment to be appropriate, and emerge with a professional opinion (known as the "auditor's report") which accompanies the statements. Officially, the statements form part of a report by the directors to the shareholders regarding their stewardship. As has been suggested, the statements circulate somewhat more widely so as to provide a generalized picture of the corporation's financial activities and position.

STAGE D: ANALYSIS

While statements provide financial data that have been interpreted by management in terms which management consider appropriate, serious investment analysts can be expected to want to do some further interpreting of their own. They may use additional information which they have collected, and they may work out comparisons with other corporations and with projections of future sales and earnings. They are free to work out any ratios which they consider efficacious. From this work, they must come to a conclusion as to whether, at their current market price, the shares of the corporation are a buy or sell.

STAGE E: DECISION

With the data provided by the analyst, the investor reaches the point of decision.

Interpretation of Financial Data

From the foregoing analysis, it may be observed that interpretation of financial data takes place at two levels: at Stage B, management carries out important judgmental work; and at Stage D, the analyst contributes his interpretations. Management, of course, must be better informed than anyone else about what is going on. They have access to all the information there is, and they are in a position to decide how data will be processed and what information is required. The outside analyst (looking in, as someone has said, "through the shop window") cannot hope to have as intimate a knowledge of the facts. He has, however, the important advantage of independence.

If you look at the whole five-stage process whereby the actual transactions of a corporation are analysed, adjusted, and refined into the ultimate data for decision-making, it becomes apparent that published financial statements are produced in the middle of that process. Some interpretations are made by management before the production of statements, and some interpretations are made subsequently by independent analysts. Thus, when management prepares a statement, there is a choice to be made with respect to how much of the interpreting they should do themselves and how much they should leave for the analyst.

My plea for more informative financial statements can be stated as a plea that management should carry the interpretation (although inevitably judgmental) farther than they do. One can recognize the advantages an analyst has as a result of his position of independence. But, important as this may be, it is outweighed by the fact that only management have access to all the underlying data. The analyst is not in this position. To take two very troublesome areas: if fixed assets and inventories are to be stated at relevant values, the work of reaching such values must start way back at the initial accounting processes. Otherwise, the information will simply never be available for the necessary calculations—regardless of how independent the analyst may be.

With regard to my plea that management carry their interpretation farther, it should also be remembered that management's interpretations at Stage B are reviewed and confirmed by the opinion of a professional auditor, whose independent status is assured by all possible means.

Brass Tacks—Attempting the Achievable

When we turn away from the theoretical aspects of the subject and get down to brass tacks, the first point we should emphasize is that no one needs to wait for the clearing-up of theoretical issues in order to start producing better statements. Management must not pretend that they are waiting for a final settlement of the theoretical arguments which are proceeding vigorously now—and which we shall always have with us. The odds are against the appearance of a modern Moses, down from the mountain, carrying tablets of stone engraved with the ultimate answers.

Improved statements can be issued immediately by any corporation. There are two, and *only* two, requirements. In the first place, the corporation must *want* to issue better statements—which is to say, more informative statements. And in the second place, the company issuing statements must accept the fact that quality in financial reporting is relative rather than absolute. What we want to produce is better statements, and we will never produce better statements if we wait until all controversy has ceased and there is general agreement on what the ideal statement should be.

The Question of How Far, How Fast?

As we turn now from theoretical discussion to a consideration of the practical steps that can be taken, it is important that we establish one principle. It is my conviction that any corporation can move immediately to a thorough-going current-value accounting. Were a corporation to do so, all assets and liabilities would be stated at current value, and the income statement would present income on this same basis. I have no reason to expect that such a change would present insuperable difficulties, and this is what I think corporation managements should now proceed to do. I have, however, a great appreciation for the bias to caution which management responsibilities tend to develop. For those who believe (as I do not) that it is necessarily safer to introduce changes slowly rather than suddenly, I would like to point out that any one (or any combination) of the many suggestions in the following pages can be adopted separately. If it seems a natural evolutionary process to proceed piecemeal, item by item, then this is better than nothing at all. But, let me repeat once more that I see no danger, and in fact nothing but advantage, in proceeding briskly across the board. (The problems of a transitional period, during which all this brilliant thinking is absorbed, are dealt with later.) What follows, then, can be accepted as a package deal—or, piece by piece. While a timid pottering with individual items is not what I recommend, it is certainly better than nothing.

A company that wants to produce better statements has, therefore, two choices. Either it can overhaul its financial statements from end to end in the light of the best current ideas, or it can select some specific problem and tackle that. Let us now consider how a company might go about an immediate improvement by selecting one particular problem. For purposes of illustration, let us start with the valuation of land. This is not usually a company's most important asset; but for purposes of illustration, it has an attractive simplicity.

Land

Normally, land is valued at cost in the balance sheet. Sometimes, perhaps usually, it is not an important item. But there have been cases in which serious scandals (and near-scandals) have resulted from the inadequacy of the cost basis in accounting for real estate. The dangers occur when a corporation has important holdings of land over a long period of years—during which time, values rise sharply. If land is carried at cost, a huge increase in value may remain undisclosed to the shareholders. It has happened, in such circumstances, that another corporation has become aware of the hidden asset and made a "takeover bid" for the shares at a price which is far too low—that is to say, at a price which ignores the enhanced value of land. In their ignorance, shareholders have sometimes accepted such bids.

Thus, we have here what is potentially a most undesirable situation. A company with important land holdings which it carries at cost can immediately produce more useful statements simply by drawing attention to the current value of the land. It should be observed that this is equally important whether or not the land has enhanced in value—because if the current value is not disclosed, the shareholders are left in ignorance as to whether or not there has been enhancement. And of course, it is just as important to know that there has *not* been enhancement as that there *has* been.

Let us now consider the different ways in which this additional information might be disclosed. Three methods suggest themselves.

1) The simplest method of all is to note on the financial statements that the value of land, in the opinion of management, is such and such. A note can be quite descriptive—for example, it might explain that management's opinion is based on recent sales of properties which management considers comparable in value. Such a note is surely better than nothing—or, to put it at the very lowest, is at least as good as nothing. The shareholder must decide the extent to which he wishes to rely on management's opinion on land values. If he has doubts about the validity of management's opinion, at least he is on warning that there might be an enhancement. The only possible objection is that some incautious shareholder may rely, to his cost, on a poor or fraudulent opinion. Unfortunately, this cannot be completely

guarded against, since no financial statement can be produced by which the gullible or unknowledgeable cannot find some way of being misled.

2) It would be better if a note were added to the financial statements giving the value of the land as appraised by a competent and independent professional appraiser. Possible objections here are that this sort of thing costs some money and the frequency of appraisals are a matter for judgment. However, a reasonably current appraisal is still more informative than cost many years ago. Moreover, as cost is given too, it is impossible that the statements be considered inferior through the inclusion of a note which shows appraisal value.

3) A still further step is to incorporate an estimated current value (however calculated) into the body of the financial statements. This produces what is potentially a much greater improvement than simply mentioning the value in a note. It makes it necessary to reflect the increase or decrease in value (if any) in the shareholder's equity. This adjustment can be made either through current earnings or through retained earnings, or it can be carried to a special balance-sheet caption which describes its nature.

As to which of these methods is most appropriate, there can be considerable argument. But we must not be diverted at this point. If the estimated current value is incorporated in the statements, it is naturally necessary to show the cost of the land in a note so that a shareholder can compare the company statement with those of other companies.

There is also the further possibility of producing statements in columnar form, showing the cost base in one column and the current value in the other. This is recommended in the *Report of The American Accounting Association Committee* mentioned in the last chapter, but it is hardly my favourite method. It produces, in my opinion, an unnecessarily confusing form of presentation.

At any rate, whatever the technique used to disclose the current value, we have at least achieved our basic objective of producing a statement which is somewhat more useful, and therefore somewhat better.

In the interests of simplicity, many refinements have been ignored in the foregoing discussion. There are many things that could be done to make the information more useful still. For example, take the case of a company which owns a factory in an area where land prices have risen spectacularly. Usually, this occurs when the character of a neighbourhood changes, and the point is sometimes reached at which an area becomes too valuable to be used as a factory site. In such cases, it may be to the advantage of a company to sell its land and build its factory in more suitable surroundings. Where land is held under these conditions, it would be useful to the shareholder to have some estimate of the cost of moving the factory—since any profit on the sale of land would be offset by the costs of moving. It would be better, therefore, for the information about moving and rebuilding costs to be disclosed. This indicates the sort of improvements that can be made in financial statements once one is determined to improve them. In turn, each refinement can usually be further refined.

The Value of Experimentation

If this kind of experimentation were to become more common, more and more companies might be tempted to venture improved forms of presentation—and the law of survival of the fittest would tend to operate. If one company produced a better presentation of land values, other companies might be moved to do even better—and eventually those concerned with financial statements would get to recognize and follow improvements. Eventually, individual improvements would gain general acceptance. Then, when general acceptance of a particular improvement had been achieved, it would be time to incorporate the improvement into our code of generally accepted ground rules. Until this stage is reached, however, we would have to recognize a transition period in which the older form of information would be provided for comparative purposes.

The approach, suggested above, for better presentation of land value could be made to all other assets. Some of these assets present much more complex problems, and these will be discussed in later chapters. For the moment, let us simply emphasize the point that improved statements can be issued immediately by any company that wants to provide more information about the estimated fair current value of its assets or any part of them. This might be more useful to statement-users—and certainly could not be less useful, so long as information in the old form was also published.

Paralleling the improvement in presenting asset values, there are changes which could be adopted to make the liability side of the balance sheet more meaningful. Here again, no one need wait for the end of the accounting arguments. They have simply to consider what types of liability they are not now reporting. As on the asset side, this can be corrected specifically or by a general review of the entire company's operation.

Object of the Exercise

If we have an estimate of the current value of all assets and an estimate of all liabilities, the shareholder at least has before him as realistic a picture as he can be given of the net-asset value of his company—a figure of capital significance. Moreover, when the net-asset value has been achieved, it becomes possible to state net income properly. The increase in net-asset value during a period gives a basic figure which can then be analysed. (The form of the analysis is not under discussion here; we will go into this in a later chapter.)

Case History

It is when one gets down to cases that the need for current values is demonstrated. Suppose for example that Company X buys a tract of land for $1,000,000, intending to relocate one of its plants. This transaction may be mentioned in the annual report of the directors in the year in which it occurs—or it may not, depending on the importance of the transaction and of other things that have happened during the year. It may happen that the company does not actually build on this land, but carries it with its ordinary fixed assets at cost. This state of affairs may continue for a period of years. The transaction may escape notice entirely, or some bright investment analyst may find out about it and ask questions. If he does ask questions, he will be given various reasons why the property is continuing to be held: "Plans to relocate the plant have been temporarily held up, but are expected to be completed any day"; "This is the only land in the locality that still has possibilities of a railway siding, and it is therefore being retained for future development"; and so on. There are a hundred-and-one plausible reasons explaining why it makes sense to continue to hold the land.

Let us suppose that Company X is under the management of Mr. *A* as president. (Readers of accounting texts will recognize *A* as a man of great experience in these matters.) In due course, *A* is succeeded by *B*. On taking over the management of Company X, *B* will undoubtedly find things in a much worse state of confusion than he had expected. This always happens. What results is usually described as a new broom sweeping clean—although it is doubtful whether new brooms actually sweep any cleaner than old brooms. However, the new president of a company always discovers problems. It is just like buying a new house from someone—an occurrence which always results in your wife's finding places to dust where the previous owner's wife didn't. It is factors such as this which are a necessary part of preventing one from losing one's self-esteem entirely.

In any event, B eventually discovers that Company X is holding a bit of land which it does not need and which is worth a good deal less than it cost. If he inquires deeply enough into the history of the case, he may discover that under A's regime, far too much was paid for the land. Or, if he is too busy, he may simply conclude that land in the area has deteriorated in value. He will probably find that there are, in point of fact, many other tracts of land with good railway siding possibilities; or he may come to realize that railway sidings are not important to the company. In any event, let us say that the net result is that he finds that the company has been paying taxes on a useless bit of property. He decides to sell it, and finds that he can only get $100,000 for it. By good planning, however, he eventually contrives to get some developer interested in the property and sells it for $300,000.

B has done admirably for the company. And yet the net result in the financial statements is the sudden appearance of a loss of $700,000 on sale of property. This sort of thing gets interpreted along somewhat the following lines:

FIRST INVESTOR: I see that Company X earned $1.85 last quarter. It looks to me as if it might be a good buy. Earnings seem to be coming along nicely since B took over management.

SECOND INVESTOR: Earnings look all right, but I sometimes wonder whether B has quite A's touch in financial transactions. They apparently lost $700,000 last year in real estate deals.

While the utter unfairness of this kind of comment is manifest, it results from the sort of misunderstanding that is bound to develop under present accounting methods. For example, if land values had risen (instead of declined) because of a residential development that was quite unforeseen when the land was purchased as a factory site, exactly the opposite impression would have been created when it was sold. B would then have been regarded as having a very sure touch in these matters—a conclusion that is equally unjustifiable.

This kind of illustration not only indicates the inadequacy of the cost basis for fixed assets, it also throws some light on the essential nature of the accounting process. Of course, when one sets up a simple illustration of this sort, it is not possible to get the whole flavour of actual investment judgments. For instance, it might be assumed that some kind of disclosure of the facts in a case like this would keep people from being misled. However, this is not usually possible. In practice, nothing ever happens quite so simply as *A*'s regime going out and *B*'s coming in. Large corporations are managed by groups of executives, each of whom participates in decisions in an indefinable manner—as anyone soon finds out when he tries to trace the blame for some misguided decision.

What we are attempting to do when we produce an annual balance sheet and income account is to provide a summing up of all the multitudinous activities started, continued, completed, or abandoned during a given year. Thus, the whole problem in accounting is to convert various types of assets and liabilities into a common denominator, so that they can then be added and subtracted. For it is only by this means that we can end up with a composite overall picture—the sort of picture provided by the net-asset position and net income on operations. Therefore, it is no answer to criticisms of the cost method to say that supplementary information can be given which will explain any individual items that are considered important enough to require mention. In preparing his statements, the accountant sets out with the sole purpose of giving a summarized overall view.

*   *   *

Once we recognize the tentative nature of financial statements, we will appreciate that there is no need to become bogged down in theoretical discussions. Such discussions are good, and through them we can go on developing still further improvements. But there is no need to wait for a conclusion of any discussion before going into action. In the present chapter we have dealt at some length with the relatively simple case of land valuation. In succeeding chapters, we will consider some of the more complex problems presented by other types of asset.

CHAPTER 10

Buildings, Machinery, and Equipment

While I have suggested that a statement which contains some reference to the current value of land (however vague that estimate might be) is more useful than a statement which contains no reference at all, clearly it would be a somewhat limited achievement if statement reform did not go beyond this point. After all, for a great many corporations, land is not a significant factor.

In considering what steps should be taken toward improved statements, land was selected to start with because it demonstrates several things clearly. In the first place, if one accepts the idea that making statements more useful is our sole objective, then improvements can be made immediately. In the second place, the illustration of land emphasizes the fact that procedures are not of supreme importance. If one sets out with the right objective, procedures will look after themselves. The third important point (and a point which I hope was also illustrated in the previous chapter) is the need for leadership in producing better statements. Every improvement, no matter how simple, has to be pioneered by someone. The hope is that others will follow. If we could ever get the notion across that improvements are easy and yet important, perhaps we could develop an atmosphere in which corporations vied with one another to find new and useful refinements. If this atmosphere were ever created, our problems would not be solved immediately—but they would get solved eventually.

Land afforded a simple illustration of the principles of statement reform—principles which are applicable to all assets. For various reasons, though, some types of asset present special difficulties. I now propose that we discuss several of these more involved cases.

Tangible Fixed Assets

Land is classified by accountants under the heading of "tangible fixed assets," a heading which also covers such important assets as buildings, machinery, and equipment. In the present chapter, we deal with these other categories. (Later, we will tackle the even more puzzling area which accountants describe as "intangible fixed assets.")

To begin with, the term "fixed assets" is not a particularly felicitous one. The implication is that the assets are permanent. In the case of land, this is perhaps literally true, because though land may be eroded, or lose its fertility, or have its top soil removed, such things happen only in special circumstances. In the normal situation, one may assume the permanent existence of land. Changes in the value of land generally come slowly and through changing economic conditions. The accounting problems are thus relatively simple when compared with those encountered in accounting for buildings, machinery, or equipment.

The added complication that is introduced when considering buildings, machinery, and equipment is this: as these assets actually wear out, it would be absurd to account for them on an assumption of permanent existence. Moreover, such assets not only wear out, they are also likely to be subject to much more violent and frequent fluctuations in value—through changes in fashion, through the production of annual models, or as the result of new technology. Thus, buildings, machinery, and equipment are subject to all the variations to which land is subject—*plus* many others.

The accountant's approach to tangible fixed assets has developed from his preoccupation with transactions. Wherever possible, he has built on the basic concept of recording receipts and disbursements. Normally, disbursements apply to the period in which they occur. This would go for the payment of wages and most expenses, for the purchase of goods, and for most other transactions that have to be accounted for. However, the purchase of a building clearly relates, not to the current period, but to a period of years over which the building can be expected to last and to contribute to the earning of revenue.

The Amortization Concept (Depreciation)

Thus, to the accountant, a fixed asset is simply an acquisition that is expected to last longer than one financial period. Statements would be meaningless if the expenditures made in acquiring such assets were charged off as expense against the revenue of the current period—so the accounting solution is logical and reasonable enough. An estimate is made of the useful life of the building, and its cost is charged off over this useful life. This procedure involves the introduction of a number of estimates: there is the basic estimate of useful life; and, once this is established, there are a great variety of ways in which the expenditure can be written off over such estimated life. Simplest of all is the so-called straight-line method where a building which is expected to last fifty years is charged off at the rate of two percent per year. There are variations on this theme (all completely arbitrary) and most of them are aimed at writing off larger portions of the building's cost in its earlier years—since these are assumed to be its most useful years. For certain classes of assets, such as motor vehicles, there is another approach which assumes that cost is best written off on a usage basis. Thus, an automobile may be written off on the basis of so much per mile—rather than so much per year. As indicated above, all of these methods are basically arbitrary.

In determining which procedure is to be used in writing off the cost of fixed assets, there are (as has been already implied) two basic factors: firstly, physical wear and tear; and secondly, obsolescence. The latter may occur when better methods of production reduce the cost of a machine or when new inventions render it obsolete. In most cases, the element of wear and tear is somewhat predictable. The factor of obsolescence is much more difficult to deal with. It is clearly impossible to predict the rate at which new inventions will render old machinery obsolete, or at which new products will make those owned suddenly valueless.

In conventional accounting, then, fixed assets are normally carried in the balance sheet at original cost less amounts amortized—although it is permissible, in some circumstances, to carry such assets at appraised value, so long as the fact that they are so carried is clearly disclosed. In any event, the term "fixed assets" is inappropriate. Something like "long-term assets" would be more accurate.

The Application of Current Values

In principle, the approach to current valuation of fixed assets is quite straightforward. Any expenditures which benefit only the current period are written off—and that's that. This applies not only to articles which are actually consumed, but also to expenditures which may benefit more than one period, but which are quite immaterial and therefore can be immediately expensed without distorting financial statements. Expenditures of any significance which are expected to benefit future periods represent value at the end of the year and must be assessed if a proper balance sheet is to be produced.

The point is that a corporation which enters a new financial period owning a machine which is still useful has an advantage over someone who is starting from scratch and who must therefore purchase such a machine. This usefulness is the "value" which the accountant must attempt to measure. Having calculated an appropriate value to carry forward, the accountant has, by the same operation, established the proper charge to income for the old period—as everything must be written off except the amount which it is reasonable to carry forward.

The fact that a company owning a machine which it will use to earn future profits is in a better position than a company without such a machine is, of course, self-evident. This is demonstrated when one corporation sets out to buy another. Consider the common case of a corporation's wanting to enter a new field—either geographically or in product line. Such a corporation can always set up a new company from scratch. It simply obtains a charter, puts up a certain amount of money (perhaps arranges other financing), collects an appropriate staff, and sets about developing its manufacturing and merchandising facilities. But this procedure is time-consuming, and thus expensive. As an alternative, the corporation can purchase a company that is already established in business. It may thus get off to a flying start, and it is worth paying something to achieve this. We come now to the really crucial question: *How much* is it worth paying in order to get this flying start? The answer to this question provides the ideal accounting value. The net-asset value and earning power of a company should be stated at the amount which a willing (but not desperate) buyer would pay for the company; and this amount would, in turn, depend on what the purchaser estimated it would cost him to develop similar facilities from scratch. The question of whether it is best to start afresh or to buy another company depends (abnormal situations apart) on which would be the least expensive way to achieve what one wants.

Anyone who makes a serious calculation of what price he should pay for a company must place a reasonable value on each of the assets that he will be acquiring and on each of the liabilities that he will be taking over. In effect, he must produce his own balance sheet for the business, based on asset values which he regards as being realistic. Depending on how methodical his approach is, he may actually go through the net-asset calculation in a systematic way (producing in reality a new balance sheet), or he may simply make some rough calculations to bring book values into line with reality. But in either event, it is essentially the same process of calculating what the various things he is purchasing are worth to him—i.e., their current value. In order to produce such a balance sheet, he will, among other things, have some appraisal or estimate made of the value to him of the buildings, machinery, and equipment which he will acquire. It is this concept of value that one should strive for in valuing these assets for purposes of publishing annual statements —in other words, what would a willing purchaser give for them?

I think it is hard to argue that a person who had a balance sheet especially prepared for him to help establish what he should pay for a company would not want the assets valued on this basis. The whole thesis of this book is that the investor who buys and sells shares of a corporation is, in effect, in the same position as someone who is considering the purchase of the whole enterprise. The only difference between a corporation that is buying another company in its entirety and the investor who is purchasing a modest number of shares is that, for the corporation, the matter is liable to be important enough for it to have its accounting experts prepare a special balance sheet which values assets on a current basis. It is not likely that this will be possible for a shareholder who is intent on buying or selling a few shares. Thus, the shareholder must rely on the latest balance sheet published by the company. And it is for this reason that I maintain that such a balance sheet should be prepared as close to current economic realities as possible.

A balance sheet is not the only important consideration in these cases. Trends are also important. For example, a company which is increasing in value is worth more than one which has the same net assets but which is decreasing in value—other things being equal. However, as explained elsewhere, this gets back to the same point. Earning trends are only significant if realistically calculated—and they are not realistically calculated if they are based on the amortization of irrelevant balance-sheet values.

Depreciated Cost

Under our present accounting conventions, therefore, what would seem to be the value of buildings is simply the amount of cost which has not yet been charged off against revenue by one of our arbitrary procedures. We must examine the concept of depreciation a little more closely. Here again, the name is an unfortunate one. The term "depreciation" suggests a wearing out in value—whereas, as we have already seen, the accountant's concept is not so much a *wearing out* of values as a systematic *writing off* of original cost. The word "amortization" is a much more accurate term—as the French, who use it, remind us.

Depreciation accounting developed from our conviction that accounting should be based on cost. As we have seen, on the assumption that cost was a proper basis for fixed assets, writing off the cost over an appropriate number of financial periods seemed just what was required. This involves estimates; but if the estimates were wrong, the resulting difference could be picked up eventually as profit or loss on disposal of fixed assets.

In short, accountants have come to value buildings in much the same way that they would value a prepaid insurance policy. It is customary, in many forms of insurance, to write three-year policies, and the premiums for such policies should be written off over a period of three years. As the portion of the payment applicable to the second and third years is, in effect, paid in advance, logically a discount factor should be included in the allocation of cost to these years. But, for the sake of simplicity, the usual practice is to write off a third of the premium each year—and it is difficult to imagine a case in which the resulting distortion would be significant. Fixed-asset costs are dealt with on the same principle.

It may be noticed that in a static economy, this might be reasonable. There would inevitably be the problem of estimating useful life, but otherwise, the amortization process would be applicable. However, as we do not live in a static economy, depreciation accounting does not give us a reliable indication of value. We must take into consideration price-level changes, which are important when price levels fluctuate violently and also in times of creeping inflation (such as we have recently become accustomed to). Cost amortization is now apt to diverge so far from value (particularly for long-lived assets) that it ceases to be a satisfactory basis for accounting. Moreover, price levels are not the only things which change in our economy. New inventions make machines suddenly obsolete. And even in buildings, such developments as air conditioning and more efficient types of layout reduce the value of old buildings. Another source of change—namely, new styles and fashions— also makes the assessment of established values necessary. All these tendencies toward change make amortized cost a quite unsatisfactory basis for asset valuation.

It should be noted that depreciation, or amortization, is primarily a cost-based concept. It is simply a matter of allocating cost over a number of periods. In current-value accounting, depreciation does not necessarily play a part. The equivalent to depreciation expense in current-value statements is the change in asset value between balance-sheet dates. In the valuation process, the depreciation technique may well be useful—in that the best approach in valuing an asset might be to calculate the value of the asset new and to apply to such value an age or depreciation factor. Just as cost would be used in current-value accounting when relevant, so, and not otherwise, would depreciation be used when useful in establishing value.

Valuation Procedures

Estimating the cost of assets may be tackled in several different ways. The accountant is continuously faced with deciding which procedure is most appropriate. Quite often, an appropriate procedure will suggest itself in the light of the particular circumstance related to the asset. In other cases, several equally valid procedures may suggest themselves. It is these latter cases which give rise to the lack of uniformity which worries so many people.

Let us start with the assumption that any procedure is likely to produce, at best, only a rough approximation of value. From this, it can be argued (I think unanswerably) that uniformity of procedures for a certain type of asset is desirable—because if a company values an asset by the same procedures at the start and close of a period, it is less likely to produce an improper result than if it uses one method at the start and another at the close. If a selected procedure tends either to overstate or to understate value (that same procedure being used at both ends of the period), it will be less likely to distort income than if procedures which have opposite tendencies are used. Consistency is most important from this point of view. However, it is wrong to argue from this that there is any necessary merit in insisting on the same procedure for different types of asset. (This point was argued in detail in Chapter 6 when we were dealing with ground rules.)

We might now consider briefly some of the approaches to the valuation of such assets as buildings and machinery.

1) *Appraisal*

An appraisal may be simply done, with great accuracy, in cases where a ready market for the article exists. Normally, such equipment as typewriters or adding machines can be easily valued by reference to price lists. As some of these assets have a reasonably predictable useful life, it is quite often a simple matter to work out a formula for amortizing costs which will produce a reasonably realistic valuation. Buildings and heavy machinery must usually be appraised for insurance purposes. Sometimes, such appraisals are rather casually done; but there are independent professional appraisers who can do reliable work and who can provide a satisfactory accounting valuation.

It goes without saying that irresponsible appraisals are an attractive device to the pusher of bogus securities. Moreover, as businessmen would not be in business unless they were optimists, they frequently convince themselves (and try to convince others, all in good faith) that certain properties are far more valuable than they actually are. Thus, through the combined efforts of the fraudulent and the merely enthusiastic, appraisals have come to be regarded (particularly by honest and unenthusiastic people like accountants) with uneasiness. There are just too many poor devils who have lost their shirts relying on them.

Nevertheless, the feasibility of honest and reliable appraisals must not be dismissed simply because there have sometimes been fraudulent and irresponsibly optimistic valuations in the past. Nowadays, there are professional firms who do serious and skilful work in this field, and if more importance were given to appraisals in accounting, it is likely that we would develop improved techniques.

An example of this is provided by a manufacturing concern which has a series of somewhat similar plants scattered across the country. This company followed the standard practice of carrying plant at depreciated cost. For many years, the plants had been appraised for insurance purposes every five years. Then the comptroller of the company embarked on a study of the company's position at current value, and used the insurance appraisals in the process. He immediately noticed that two relatively similar plants were appraised at quite different values, and on looking into the matter discovered that the appraisers involved had used quite different approaches to valuation. By following the appraisal working papers through, the comptroller, though not a trained appraiser, had little difficulty in deciding which of the techniques was preferable. Naturally, all plants were appraised on the preferred method thereafter.

The moral is: if senior accounting officials were to pay more attention to appraisals, we would likely get more reliable appraisals. There is nothing very esoteric about the techniques used, and any reasonably sensible executive can, after a little inquiry, satisfy himself as to whether or not an appraisal can be relied upon.

But the case for the feasibility of appraisals need not be argued along theoretical lines. The incontestible proof that appraisals can be made satisfactorily is provided, in the most practical way, by the fact that hard-headed businessmen keep making them in the normal course of business and demonstrate their confidence in them by putting up cold hard cash. This happens each time that a corporation or an individual buys a business. No purchase could take place without the buyer's and the vendor's deciding what the enterprise is worth. There is normally a good deal of bargaining and manoeuvring for position during such deals, but the buyer must start out by deciding what the business is worth to him. This is not the price that he is likely to offer for it. In fact, he offers either the lowest figure at which he thinks the vendor might sell or an even lower "bargaining figure"—simply as a matter of tactics. Still, he must start out by deciding how much he would be prepared to pay if pressed. For example, if he decides that the business is worth $1,400,000 to him, he may start by offering $1,000,000. In subsequent horse-trading, he may allow himself to be coaxed upwards; but he must have clearly in mind a point beyond which he will not go. The only way for him to establish what this is, is by studying the business and deciding what it is worth. Depending on all sorts of circumstances, the study may vary from a fairly cursory estimate to a meticulous item-by-item review with the aid of all sorts of professional consultants. (The vendor, of course, must go through much the same sort of calculations in deciding what price he should be prepared to accept.)

The point here is that it is ridiculous to say that appraisals cannot be sufficiently reliable for accounting purposes when they are regarded as being sufficiently reliable to form the basis for laying out hard cash when a business is purchased. It really boils down to this: businessmen rely on their judgment of the current value of an enterprise because they could not carry on in any other way. They simply have to accept whatever risk is involved. As it is the accountant's job to facilitate the carrying on of business by providing the necessary basic data for making decisions, he too must produce the most useful figures he can—and if this inevitably involves some risk of error, that risk must be faced. The accountant's duty is simply to minimize this risk by making the most intelligent and careful estimates he can.

2) *Price-level adjustments*

Another possibility is to follow the procedure of amortizing cost, but to adjust original cost by a price-level index. This at least takes into consideration one important factor of change, and is an improvement on cost to that extent. There are a variety of published price indices, and interesting questions arise as to which is most appropriate. The nature of the asset will sometimes make the choice of index clear. Otherwise, government statistical services are available to explain the various indices and to recommend an appropriate one. And of course, there are also professional experts who may be consulted.

3) *Replacement cost*

This approach to valuation is based on estimating what it would cost to replace an asset at the balance-sheet date. Here again, there are a number of different ways of making the calculation. A building may be examined and an estimate made of the cost of reproducing it at current price levels. This will normally be a satisfactory procedure for fairly new buildings, unless there have been some important technological changes in the meantime which render recently-built buildings obsolete. However, for old buildings, literal replacement cost means almost nothing. Normally, no one would dream of replacing a really old building in anything like similar form. In such cases, a more useful and realistic replacement cost might be obtained by calculating the cost of replacing the old building with a modern building of equal capacity. As a matter of fact, for all general purposes, this concept of replacing capacity is probably the most useful approach to fixed-asset valuation. For many assets, it becomes quite difficult; but, where it is possible, it is likely to be the most useful approach.

4) *Realizable value*

In some instances, the price that an asset will realize can be a useful basis for determining its accounting value. Financial statements are produced on the "going concern" assumption. Thus, what a company would get for an asset on forced liquidation is not usually significant. However, cases do arise—usually where there has been a very big enhancement in value (that is, where an asset has a realizable value far higher than its value in its present use). In such cases, it may be important, in the interests of the shareholders, to sell the asset. This might happen, for example, where a factory was built in an area which later became popular for residential purposes, with a correspondingly high rise in land values. In such cases, it might be profitable to dispose of the land and rebuild a factory in some lower cost area. And if this is done, the realizable value takes on great importance—in spite of the "going concern" concept.

Accounting Treatment

When we mentioned the importance of disclosing the current value of land, it was pointed out that this could be done in two ways. Either the current value could be disclosed in a note, or it could be incorporated in the body of the financial statements—the latter being naturally the preferable treatment. The same choice is open in disclosing the current value of building and equipment. Here, however, the incorporation of current values in the regular statements is both more important and more complicated.

Under current-value accounting, the matter of first importance is the value of the asset at start and close of the accounting period. It is the difference between value at these two points which measures the gain or loss on the asset during the period. However, this gain or loss is composed of two elements, and these must be distinguished. For example, consider a factory building in time of rising prices. At the end of the year, the building has increased in value owing to the price rise, and has decreased in value by being one year older. The first of these elements is a holding gain, and the latter an operating cost.

To reflect what has happened in the accounts, we require the following entries. (1) To record the enhanced value of the building through price or market factors, the asset must be written up (*Debit*: buildings; *Credit*: shareholders' equity). (2) To record the usage cost, income should be charged with a sum representing the current value of the building amortized over its expected useful life, in the conventional manner (*Debit*: depreciation expense; *Credit*: accumulated depreciation). This should give the general idea. But there are several different ways in which the detailed accounting entries can be put through—each resulting in a somewhat different final presentation.

One extremely interesting point arises when current values have been established. Should the estimated value of the building new be set up, with a corresponding credit to some such account as "appraisal surplus"? Or should the value of the building at its current age be set up directly? In the former case, it is necessary to adjust accumulated depreciation at the start of the period so that the net value in the balance sheet will be an appropriate one. When this procedure is followed, a further question of considerable intellectual interest arises: Should the additional depreciation at the start of the period be provided by a charge against retained earnings or against appraisal surplus?

In *The Elusive Art of Accounting*, I have dealt with this particular question at full length, and it is perhaps undesirable to go over all this ground here. The important point to underline is that there are interesting difficulties and challenges in current-value accounting. These will never be resolved by theoretical discussion, but companies who push forward with the broad objective of producing more informative statements based on current values may be sure that they will find ways of coping with the problems which arise.

In this discussion, we have dealt with general rules. The variety of types of buildings, machinery, and equipment makes it difficult to cover all of the many approaches that may be used in establishing the current value of assets in these categories. However, there is no harm in the fact that such different approaches may be appropriate, so long as one sticks firmly to the essential rule—which, once again, is as follows: the value of any asset is an estimate of how much better off the company is, at a certain date, for having it.

With regard to valuation techniques, there is endless room for research into methods. If it were agreed that current values were essential, it would be inevitable that techniques for reaching current values fairly would be continuously improved. As I have emphasized elsewhere, once we have accepted the goal, we will begin to find out what our real problems are in the process of working towards such goals. Our techniques will become more and more accurate. Eventually, we will undoubtedly develop much greater capability in measuring assets than we now possess. But this will not happen unless we get started. There have been plenty of good ideas suggested which corporations that wish to produce better statements can now put into effect—and there is no reason to procrastinate.

CHAPTER 11

Inventories

Inventories are a most difficult area in accounting. The introductory problems, which we first become familiar with in accounting texts, are disarmingly simple. We find that A (good old reliable A) goes into business, buys 200 units of something at $10, and sells 150 of them at $15. Required: to prepare a profit and loss account for A—an exceedingly simple task.

150 units sold at $15	$2,250
Cost of 150 units	1,500
Profit	$ 750
Inventory carried forward (50 units at $10)	$ 500

The principle is simple and sensible. Costs which expire during a period are applied against the revenue received, and the result is profit or loss. Costs that are expected to be consumed in the following period are carried forward (constituting an asset) to be charged against the revenue of the subsequent period. Where does the complexity come in?

Value Changes

Perhaps the first factor to cope with is the tendency for goods to deteriorate in value. There are a few exceptions, such as whisky, which mature and improve with age. But most goods tend to deteriorate. More frequently still, the value of goods changes (up or down) with price movements. When this happens, the accountant cannot ignore the change in value; he must do something about it. The simple and straightforward solution would be to carry the goods forward at their current value—whether this was above or below cost. But this was not what accountants decided to do. They did recognize the necessity for reducing goods to current value if this involved a write-down; but if value increased, they were not prepared to make a corresponding write-up. This was consistent with the accountant's gloomy view of life (a view which has led him to a stoic acceptance of the role of antidote to entrepreneurial optimism) and this approach provided an acceptable solution to inventory valuation in the days when credit was the only serious problem. However, the underlying principle suffers from the fact that it is not really a principle at all, but simply an arbitrary device which is used to guard against one particular deviation in value.

Once financial statements had become more widely used (i.e., used for purposes other than credit), an interest developed in the investor's concern with growth and income measurement. For these broader purposes, the rule of "cost and market whichever is lower" makes no sense at all. It has, nevertheless, been closely adhered to in financial accounting. Thus, one of the most important reforms that we must make is to jettison this quite out-of-date maxim.

It will not be easy to persuade accountants to move from a position which they have come to think of as safe ground. It will be all the more difficult because, in a desperate attempt to make "the lower of cost and market" scientific, a great deal of sophisticated and ingenious reasoning has been aimed at elaborating the concept. The attempt to shape this rough practical rule into something that resembles a logically-based scientific principle has taken the form of longer and longer dissertations on the meaning of the terms "cost" and "market"—and all in a futile attempt to make it appear that there is some solid basis for writing down an asset when it deteriorates, but not writing it up when it increases in value.

The dilemma into which we have got ourselves by staying with cost long after its inadequacies became apparent is illustrated by our attempts to rationalize our position into what is supposed to be well worked-out doctrine. To illustrate this, I should like to comment on current pronouncements of the AICPA on inventory pricing, as set forth in *Accounting Research and Terminology Bulletins (Final Edition) 1961*. (Incidentally, I should perhaps explain that I am fond of selecting AICPA pronouncements, not because they provide an easy target, but because I am convinced that they represent the most advanced and serious pronouncements issued anywhere.) This particular pronouncement runs through nine pages of patient elaboration, but I think that my point can be made by using only a few extracts. The cost basis is established, at the outset, in these words:

> The primary basis of accounting for inventories is cost, which has been defined generally as the price paid or consideration given to acquire an asset. As applied to inventories, cost means in principle the sum of the applicable expenditures and charges directly or indirectly incurred in bringing an article to its existing condition and location.

This sounds fair enough. But in fact, it isn't. As cost is really a quite unsuitable basis for our purposes, we must immediately start hedging— as does the AICPA committee when it stipulates that:

> Cost for inventory purposes may be determined under any one of several assumptions as to the flow of cost factors (such as first-in first-out, average, and last-in first-out); the major objective in selecting a method should be to choose the one which, under the circumstances, most clearly reflects periodic income.

It should be observed that these arbitrary assumptions about cost flows introduce problems which are virtually insoluble. For example, by selecting FIFO, a corporation will produce reports that cannot be safely compared with those of corporations which use LIFO—since such comparisons may prove misleading. We have thus committed what is perhaps the worst disservice to statement-users by introducing an element of non-comparability.

It should further be observed that this gratuitous distortion does not arise under current-value accounting. If this latter concept is established as the determining rule, corporations may use FIFO if it gives the best approach to current value, but not otherwise. And the same is true of LIFO. It does not destroy comparability, in these circumstances, if one corporation is on FIFO and the other on LIFO—because in each case the result is to value inventory at the same concept of current value, and the statements will therefore be comparable. As a matter of fact, under current-value accounting, there is no need whatever to make any assumptions relating to the flow of goods through inventory. Under cost-based accounting, however, such assumptions have to be made—because we are inventorying costs, and not goods. In current value, we have goods on hand and we simply calculate what their value is. As it does not matter what they cost, the flow of cost is irrelevant.

Next, in the same bulletin of the AICPA, we find the following stipulation:

> A departure from the cost basis of pricing the inventory is required when the utility of the goods is no longer as great as its cost. Where there is evidence that the utility of goods, in their disposal in the ordinary course of business, will be less than cost, whether due to physical deterioration, obsolescence, changes in price levels, or other causes, the difference should be recognized as a loss of the current period. This is generally accomplished by stating such goods at a lower level commonly designated as "market".

This is a necessary concession. Not to insist on a write-down in such cases would be to produce quite meaningless results. But, notice that in conceding write-downs, we depart from the cherished doctrine of objectivity and get into the realm of judgment. However, we do not extend the concession, as we logically should, to write-ups in contrary cases. Thus, we have sacrificed objectivity without achieving a sensible general base.

When it finally gets around to defining "market," the AICPA committee says:

> As used in the phrase "lower of cost or market"* the term "market" means current replacement cost (by purchase or by reproduction, as the case may be) except that:
>
> (1) Market should not exceed the net realizable value (i.e., estimated selling price in the ordinary course of business less reasonably predictable costs of completion and disposal); and
>
> (2) Market should not be less than net realizable value reduced by an allowance for an approximately normal profit margin.
>
> *The terms "cost or market, whichever is lower" and "lower of cost or market" are used synonymously in general practice and in this chapter. The committee does not express any preference for either of the two alternatives.

Unfortunately, this definition introduces an unnecessary compromise by allowing a choice between (a) taking profit into consideration and (b) omitting it. Before winding up, the committee gets around (strangely, as it seems to me) to "exceptional cases," concerning which we find this interesting discussion:

> Only in exceptional cases may inventories properly be stated above cost. For example, precious metals having a fixed monetary value with no substantial cost of marketing may be stated at such monetary value; any other exceptions must be justifiable by inability to determine appro-

priate approximate costs, immediate marketability at quoted market price, and the characteristic of unit interchangeability. Where goods are stated above cost this fact should be fully disclosed.

It is generally recognized that income accrues only at the time of sale, and that gains may not be anticipated by reflecting assets at their current sales prices. For certain articles, however, exceptions are permissible. Inventories of gold and silver, when there is an effective government-controlled market at a fixed monetary value, are ordinarily reflected at selling prices. A similar treatment is not uncommon for inventories representing agricultural, mineral, and other products, units of which are interchangeable and have an immediate marketability at quoted prices and for which appropriate costs may be difficult to obtain.

The committee thereupon brings its discussion of inventory-pricing to a brisk close—disregarding completely the fact that it has just opened a Pandora's Box of troubles that cry out for answers. If gold and silver can be carried at selling price without restriction, why must "any other exceptions be justifiable by inability to determine appropriate approximate costs . . . etc."? And can the term "other products" be extended to cover all raw materials which are "interchangeable and have an immediate marketability"?

The Canadian Institute of Chartered Accountants first made its pronouncements on cost in Bulletin No. 5 of its Committee on Accounting and Auditing Research—a bulletin which bears the title, *The Meaning of the Term "Cost" as Used in Inventory Valuation*. In effect, this bulletin sanctions a variety of approaches to cost determination, but urges consistency once a method has been selected. However, the bulletin was issued in 1950, and the committee has apparently not yet made up its mind about the meaning of the term "market"—the other term which it uses when speaking of inventory valuation.

No refinement of language will ever conceal the fact that statements prepared on "the lower of cost and market" are unfair to vendor or borrower. Such statements may be thought to provide a safe guide to the purchaser or lender. But what about the purchaser who decides not to invest because the price looks too high—when in fact it isn't?

The problem in inventory valuation is basically simple. In fact, it is the same problem that we face with regard to other assets—namely, the problem of arriving at a reasonable value for transactions to take place. Difficulties arise because there are so many different kinds of inventory (each with wholly different characteristics) that it is not easy to form rules which will be generally applicable. Some of the complexities with which we must cope are described in the following paragraphs.

1) *Various markets*

In dealing with marketable securities, the problem is a great deal simpler, because there is only one market for the securities. There are minor differences in the price of "board lots" and "odd lots"; and one can argue whether securities should be valued at closing bid or at the last sale price. But these are minor matters and rarely create problems. When we come to commodities, a more complicated situation is encountered. Here, there are several sale prices: price to the consumer, price to the retailer, price to the wholesaler, and so on. A wholesaler may find that his selling price changes while goods are in his possession, but this does not necessarily mean that an adjustment is indicated in the value of his inventory. The value of his inventory should not be based on his selling price (except in special cases, which are mentioned later) but should be based on his purchase price—which may or may not move with his selling price. To select the right market, we therefore reach the rule that we should adjust inventory values whenever purchase prices change.

2) *Market adjustments*

To continue with the previous comparison, marketable securities are generally assumed to be marketable unless there is some special restriction. For such securities in a company other than an investment company, the normal assumption is that they are held as a temporary reserve of cash, and it is not necessary to make the assumption that they will be liquidated during the following period. With goods in inventory, the situation is quite different. Inventories are not normally held as a reserve of cash; they are held to be sold in the following period. Here enter questions of marketability which can be quite complicated.

The price at which goods may be expected to sell depends, to some extent at least, on the quantities on hand. If normal quantities are held, the reasonable assumption is that they can be liquidated in the normal course of business without affecting the market price. However, if one is overstocked, it may be more reasonable to assume that price reductions will be necessary in order to "move" the goods. In such cases, it is reasonable to require that the value at which the goods are carried forward should be reduced.

To establish the appropriate write-down, several procedures can be adopted. One may go on the assumption, for example, that a certain percentage of gross profit should be expected. If it is estimated that the selling price will have to be reduced, the inventory value is correspondingly reduced—so that the goods, when sold, will earn this normal gross profit percentage. Another possible assumption, perhaps not usually quite so supportable, is that a certain dollar value of gross profit should be maintained on each unit. In such cases, the inventory value is reduced so that the goods can be expected to return a "normal" dollar profit per unit.

As can be imagined, many complexities may be encountered in trying to show the fairest picture. But the basic principle remains simple. The inventory should be valued at what it is worth to a going concern at the balance-sheet date.

3) *Perishability*

Another important consideration enters with goods that are perishable. These must be sold promptly, and marketability becomes a matter of overwhelming importance. This presents, however, simply the problem discussed under the previous heading—but in a highly intensified form. The same principle of valuation applies.

4) *Style*

Other goods are subject to changes in style. These may be either regular and rhythmical (as in cases where annual models are produced) or may be wayward and unpredictable. Style is a complicating factor which no one can expect to measure exactly; but, with the basic principle reiterated several times previously, some sort of appropriate valuation may be reached.

Goods which are produced in ranges of annual models do present a serious complication. Frequently, the *model* year does not coincide with the *financial* year of the corporation. If, for example, a corporation with a December 31 year-end adopts a model year which starts on April 1, it encounters the problem of valuing the "old" models on hand at December 31 at an appropriate price.

If new models are produced annually, one tough problem is to sustain sales volume throughout the whole year. Naturally, a new model is sought after more eagerly when it first comes out. This happens, not only because it is up to date, but also because the introduction of annual models tends to be accompanied by an intensive sales campaign.

The company's object should be, presumably, to maximize profits over the year. It follows from this that it is normally good business to sell the models at a higher price during the early months of issue and to gradually reduce the price so that sales will continue throughout the year. Towards the end of the year, with new models about to come out, a considerably lower sales price may be required. In our example of a company with a financial year at December 31 and a model year of April 1, the company will normally have a number of models in inventory at the end of its financial year—and these it must move before the new models come on the market. This will involve an estimate of how far prices must be reduced to effect this.

If the company carries its inventory throughout the year at the same figure of cost, it will appear to make large profits in the early months of the model year (at which time prices are high) and low profits, or even losses, during the closing months of the model year (at which time prices must be reduced). Thus, if the company's program is to maximize profits over the whole model year, statements which appear to make the operation profitable in early months and unprofitable later on obviously depart from reality.

The only proper approach to valuing goods which are subject to a model year is to regard the whole year's operation as an exercise in project accounting. To start with, an estimate is made of the price reductions that will be required during the year, and from this a total revenue for the line may be calculated. Comparing this with cost of production, we arrive at an estimated total profit during the year—and from this we can calculate an average profit per unit. With this basic information, we are then able to value our inventory at the close of each month in a realistic fashion. The inventory value will fall gradually during the model year, but will always result in a "normal" profit each month—and this is what we are trying to obtain when we attempt to find the most realistic current value for an asset. In such cases, actual sales rarely conform exactly to forecast, and there is the further complication of adjusting the original program in the light of revised forecasts. But, however difficult the calculations may be, there is a clear objective to work to—namely, the current valuation of goods on hand.

5) *Technical obsolescence*

Another vagary in inventory valuation is the possibility of technical obsolescence. A new invention (coming, frequently, quite out of the blue) can suddenly reduce the value of the company's inventory by making it obsolete. This is a factor that is almost impossible to tackle in an accounting way, because the development of some new process can never be predicted or counted upon. However, technical obsolescence is also an example of the sort of danger which any company must learn to live with so long as it carries forward inventories. And if it is to stay in business, a company must have inventories. It therefore runs a risk which cannot be measured even approximately. This illustrates the situation, which often arises, where the accountant must either ignore the risk as unmeasurable or make some arbitrary adjustment as a concession to it.

6) *Manufacturing*

When we move from a merchandising to a manufacturing company, we encounter other complexities. Everyone who is familiar with cost accounting knows the many arbitrary aspects of this subject.

It seems fairly self-evident that the direct material, direct labour, and direct overhead which go into the manufacture of goods will be part of their cost. But when we depart from these direct factors and consider indirect overhead, the situation is much less clear. Prorations of overhead over the multitudinous products of a large modern corporation must often be arbitrary—and, at times, completely without scientific justification. Nevertheless, such factors cannot be ignored without producing all sorts of anomalies.

Whatever the problem, and however arbitrary some of the assumptions must be, if we are to provide meaningful statements, we must include all overhead in inventory. On the belief that such prorationing is bound to be debatable, some companies have welcomed direct costing (as it is called), which values goods only at the direct labour and material content. This has some attractions for tax purposes, since it leads to deferral of income tax. But it notably fails to comply with our basic criterion of using values which reflect economic realities fairly from the point of view of buyers and sellers.

7) *Price-level changes*

Probably most goods carried in inventory are subject to fluctuations in price level, and these should not be ignored in arriving at a fair inventory price. Price-level changes can sometimes be established by direct market quotations. Where this is impossible, at least some reliable index number may be selected by which to adjust the price towards current market levels.

8) *Special cases*

Beyond the complexities outlined above, there is an infinite number of special cases. For example, joint products represent a problem. When a hog is slaughtered, the packing house divides the carcass into a number of cuts. On the assumption that it wishes to maximize the total return on the carcass, it must sell these cuts at various prices—the more desirable cuts going for higher prices, and the less attractive for lower prices. Now there is no way of demonstrating that the less attractive cuts are cheaper to produce than the more attractive. But, to value inventory realistically, the packing house must find some way of differentiating in value between high-quality and low-quality meat.

It is cases like this which require the development of special techniques. For example, in the case of joint costs, it is possible to work backwards from selling price to reach an inventory value which bears some relation to economic reality.

These various complexities have been listed in order to give some indication of the difficulties that enter into inventory valuation. Probably no one can really appreciate what a variety of problems obtrude themselves unless he has been personally involved in trying to work out satisfactory inventory values. But it is equally clear that all such problems can be settled, in a more or less satisfactory manner, by sticking to the basic principle that any asset should be valued by estimating the economic advantage of owning it at the balance-sheet date. With this essential yardstick, all difficulties can be overcome more or less completely.

Part of our confusion about inventory valuation derives from the fact that we are inclined to think of inventories in terms of stocks of physical goods which are carried forward at the year end. From an accounting point of view, the reality of the situation is not that certain physical goods are being carried forward, but that certain values are being carried forward in the accounts. These are values which it is appropriate to charge off against revenue of the succeeding period. Thus, the amount carried forward is the amount which there is a reasonable expectation of recovering, with normal profitability, during the following period.

Valuation from Sales Price

As several of the above cases indicate, an appropriate inventory value may be estimated in one of two ways—either by working forward from cost and adjusting this suitably, or by working backwards from an estimated selling price. The former method probably appeals to the logic of accountants, who are brought up with an historical approach to statements. However, working backwards from an estimated sales price may prove a more useful technique in some cases. And of course, where it does prove more useful, it should be resorted to.

The approach through estimated sales value is useful in a number of different circumstances. For example, it is notably popular among retailers. Most retail stores carry an infinite variety of goods, and each of these goods must be given a sales price. Moreover, this sales price must be adjusted from time to time in accordance with the demands of the market, and this is, in itself, a rather complicated task. It would be extremely onerous to work out a parallel system of costs for all goods in stock, as this would necessitate simultaneous adjustments of the cost price each time that the sales price was altered. Thus, to avoid the tremendous clerical costs of cost-pricing, retail stores tend to value their inventory at sales price less a percentage calculated to represent normal gross profit.

The important point to remember here is that whether we are working forward from cost or backward from sales, essentially the same goal is achieved—namely, that of matching revenues and expenses—or, in other words, allocating expenses to the period in which they either give rise to revenue or expire.

The Recognition of Profit

As far as revenue and expenses go, the matter is quite straightforward. You could not expect to produce a sensible financial statement for a given period unless the revenue for the period was included along with all the expenses laid out to earn such revenue. However, there is a special problem regarding profit on goods in inventory. The question here is whether we should consider profit as being realized in the period in which sale takes place or in the period in which purchase takes place.

While the normal accounting procedure is to assume that profits should be shown in the period in which sale takes place, this may not always appear to be the most sensible assumption. For example, when goods are manufactured in one period and sold in the next, it may seem plausible to argue that any resulting profit should be attributed to the year in which the goods were manufactured. If you have to choose between the relative importance of the manufacturing process and the selling process, it is understandable that some people might conclude that the manufacturing process is more important—and that the period in which manufacture takes place should therefore be credited with the profit. This is the point of view expressed by the irate production manager who complains: "We make the whole damn' contraption! All the sales people do is wrap it up and shove it across the counter!" And in fact, there would be no particular difficulty in allocating profit on goods in inventory to the period of manufacture. This could be accomplished by our inventory pricing, and this procedure has indeed been advocated by competent and serious authorities—for example, Moonitz and Sprouse in *AICPA Research Study No. 3*.

There is no way of deciding this question on the basis of logic. If we are to get the matter settled, we must do so on the basis of common sense—and from this point of view, the general rule that "profit accrues when the sale is made" seems sensible to me. Bear in mind that we are trying to give the investor a picture of the position he would buy into, and we are trying to state the assets of a company for this purpose as though it were going to compete with other companies. Thus, what is really important are the future prospects—and to estimate these properly, we should carry forward all assets at prices which would place the company on an equal position with competitors.

If profit were taken up in the year of manufacture, we would be presenting a balance sheet which included goods that would show no profit on subsequent sale—and this would surely be confusing to the purchaser of shares. It would be more natural, to my mind, to value the goods on a basis which would permit the purchaser to assume that a reasonable profit would be earned when they are sold. Another way of looking at this problem is to think of a very simple case and observe the difference between valuing inventory at cost price and at sale price. Take the merchant who has in inventory something which cost him $20 and which he intends to sell at $30. To me, it does not make any sense to place a value of $30 on a product which he could actually replace for $20. I don't think that this would be necessarily illogical; but I do think that it would be silly.

The Inevitable Exceptions

That the general rule of recognizing profits in the year of sale is a purely arbitrary decision (i.e., a decision dictated by common sense rather than by logic) is borne out by the fact that there are instances in which the rule does not appear to make good sense. For example, in the case of a long-term contract which will be worked on over a period of years, it does not make sense for profit not to be taken up until the conclusion of the contract. If such contracts are an important part of a company's business (as indeed they often are), it will be possible for the company to operate very successfully for several years without showing any profit —and to then show a very large profit in a year that is not exceptionally good, but during which a number of long-term contracts are closed out. Since this does not make sense, several methods have been devised to provide a more intelligible picture. These methods are all based on the idea of taking up, each year, a proportion of the profit which is estimated to reflect that portion of the contract which has been completed.

Another type of exception is that of instalment sales. In this case, the spreading out of payments is sometimes so important that a company which sells on an instalment basis is really in two businesses: a selling business and a financing business. In such cases, methods have been worked out whereby profit is picked up, not when the goods are sold, but over the period in which instalment payments are received. This illustrates once again the principle that recognizing profit at time of sale is a purely conventional device—normally making good sense, but subject to variation when it doesn't.

What Kind of Cost?

When balance-sheet values are calculated by working forward from costs, many problems are encountered. We have already noted the tendency in some cases to disparage overhead as an element in inventory value solely because it can only be allocated arbitrarily to individual products. But, even if it is an element that is not easily measured, it is at least an element—and we must measure it as best we can. The coal burnt in the powerhouse of a furniture company enters into the final product just as indubitably as the wood from which the furniture is made. The fact that one raw material is consumed while the other one remains identifiable is quite irrelevant. This illustration indicates the necessity of concentrating, not on physical qualities, but on financial expenditures and value changes.

It is also important, when working forward from cost in inventory valuation, to use normal costs—or, as they are usually called by accountants, "standard" costs. For example, if it is normal to spend $100 of labour in producing a certain product, and if, through some mistake or through poor performance, an item requires $150 of labour, that item should appear in the inventory on the basis of $100 of labour content—which is the estimate of what labour should have cost. To do otherwise is to penalize the future for the mistakes of the past. In a set of financial statements which are to be used as a basis for decisions affecting the future, the mistakes of the past must be buried in the past—and not carried forward. Most large corporations now have standard costing techniques which enable them to make such adjustments quite simply.

Where valuations are determined by working back from sales price, it is important to deduct the estimated costs of disposal—i.e., costs such as sales commissions, warehousing, shipping expenses, etc. From the resulting net proceeds, an amount should also be deducted for the estimated profit (as explained above). This may be achieved either by establishing a percentage of gross profit and deducting that, or by deducting the net profit plus estimated selling expenses. Either procedure should have the same result.

We must remember, in all this confusion, to keep in mind the importance of valuing inventory with an eye on competition. A few simple rules might perhaps be mentioned as a recap:

1) Use the method of calculation or procedure which is best suited to the goods being valued.

2) Use the same method consistently for each type of goods in the inventory; but do not worry about differences between types of goods, so long as each type is valued by the method which is most appropriate to its nature.

3) The main object is to be fair to both sides—the purchaser and the seller, the borrower and the lender. Naturally, personal relationships with either side should not enter into the picture. We should attempt to achieve that fine degree of detachment which Adam Smith recommended to tax collectors when he warned them that they must not "aggravate the burden on an obnoxious contributor."

The whole question of inventory valuation may sound complicated and difficult in a theoretical discussion—and in actual fact, it is. However, this does not seem a good enough reason to continue to base inventory valuation on the completely illogical basis of "lower of cost and market"—particularly in view of the fact that this illogical basis is subject to the same complexities and difficulties that would be encountered in attempting to reach a fair current value. By sticking with our present basis, we do not manage to avoid any difficulties; instead, we encounter them and still end up with a dubious result.

CHAPTER 12

Intangibles

An interesting but particularly confusing section of the balance sheet is the section devoted to what accountants describe as "intangible fixed assets." Actually, this is not much of a term for the assets in question, since what is meant, really, is "non-current assets"—excluding land, building, machinery, and such palpable and tangible assets as these. The description "long-term" is not particularly suitable either, as many of these assets do not have a term. A great variety of assets fall into the area of intangible fixed assets—including patents, copyrights, brand names, and heavenly-sounding goodwill.

Goodwill

To an accountant, goodwill means the ability to earn profits in excess of what might be considered "normal." It is, in effect, the residual value which is presumed to exist after all other assets (which are separately accounted for) have been taken into consideration. The presumption of its existence is that more profits have been earned than would have been expected from the other assets set forth in the balance sheet. It is, thus, an indication that undisclosed asset values exist. Under our present accounting conventions, the undisclosed value which may be inferred from excess earnings is made up of two elements: firstly, assets which get left out of the balance sheet because they cannot be measured; and, secondly, the understated value (sanctioned by generally accepted accounting principles) of those assets which are included. While the total of undisclosed values may be estimated by a calculation that is based on excess earnings, the portion of this which is attributable to sanctioned understatements cannot be estimated—and there is, therefore, no way of estimating a value for the undisclosed assets. Right here, we may observe one great advantage of the system which is recommended in this book. If all measurable assets are stated at the closest approximation to current value, and if unmeasurable assets are excluded entirely, then a higher than normal rate of earnings could be considered attributable to the assets that are excluded as unmeasurable—and this would give at least some notion of the value of the latter.

Measurability

It goes without saying that there are many assets, or favourable factors, that a corporation possesses for which no attempt is made to account. For example, to have a particularly fine staff is a great advantage to a company; but only the most tentative experiments (one of which will be discussed later) have been made towards measuring the value of this particular kind of asset.

When we say that such factors are unmeasurable, what we really mean is that satisfactory measuring techniques have not yet been developed for them. Even the vaguest of the intangible assets must get "valued," after a fashion, whenever a business is purchased. There may not be the methodically documented support that is needed for the kind of valuation which accountants consider proper. But nevertheless, when a company is bought, someone pays money for these factors—along with the other assets acquired. As explained previously (in connection with the valuation of inventories), precisely the same situation exists when the shares of a corporation are purchased as when the corporation is bought outright—lock, stock, and barrel. Every time that shares of a corporation change hands on the stock market, someone has, however inexplicitly, made a judgment about the value of all the company's assets —whether those assets are measurable or not.

We have already dealt with such assets as land, building, machinery, equipment, and inventories, and have found many unsatisfactory aspects in the way in which these assets are treated for accounting purposes— the basic trouble usually being a concentration on cost instead of on value. But, however unsatisfactory the treatment of such assets may be, they are at least subjected to a systematic accounting treatment. There is justifiable concern about comparability between corporations and about consistency of principle; but a great deal of thinking has been devoted to these assets, and we have emerged with a form of accounting that is at least reasonably methodical. When we come to intangibles, however, we enter a much more tangled jungle. There has been a good deal written (mainly from an academic standpoint) about accounting for intangibles —but it remains a relatively neglected area.

As an example of the cavalier treatment which this subject usually receives, it is interesting to notice that the CICA handbook (which devotes 28 pages to accounting for income taxes) dismisses intangibles in four brief paragraphs. These paragraphs read, in their entirety, as follows:

> The major items among the intangible assets should be shown separately, e.g., goodwill, franchises, patent rights, copyrights, and trade marks.
> The basis of valuation for each type of intangible asset should be disclosed. Where an intangible asset has been acquired other than through payment of cash or its equivalent, the basis of valuation should be fully described as, for example, "at cost, being the value assigned to shares issued therefor".
> Where amortization has been deducted in arriving at the carrying value of the intangible asset, this fact should be disclosed.
> The amount charged for amortization of intangible assets for the current period should be disclosed. Disclosure of the basis of amortization would be desirable.

Obviously, problems have tended to be avoided, or given up, rather than being seriously explored. This may be partly because intangibles are generally thought of as being less important than other types of assets, partly because they present virtually insoluble difficulties, and partly because they are not frequently purchased and are therefore not often encountered by the accountant in his unremitting task of analysing, classifying, and coping with transactions.

Furthermore, one may hazard the guess that the neglect of intangibles arises, to some extent, from a feeling that that which is intangible is, somehow or other, unreal. I suppose that we are all inclined to attribute reality more readily to things which are solid and can be touched. However, if we are to reach intelligent conclusions on financial reporting, we must rid ourselves of the idea that tangibility (or the lack of it) is of any significance in accounting. Many very valuable assets are intangible. We need only mention such vitally important and clearly valuable assets as marketable securities or accounts receivable. These assets are intangible in the ordinary sense of the word—but they represent claims or rights to money, and their value may be much more real than that ascribed to a solid but obsolete bit of machinery. Even land, the most palpable and indestructible asset imaginable, may not only be valueless, but may have the negative value of a liability—as we see each time that real estate is auctioned off to meet back taxes. As we noted when considering inventories, the accountant is interested in values, and not in physical qualities. When he says that he is using the "first in, first out" method of accounting for inventories, he does not mean that he is making any assumption about the physical flow of goods (in this case, that the goods purchased first are sold first). He is referring instead to the flow of costs, and "first in, first out" is simply a convention whereby earlier costs are matched against sales before later costs.

The insubstantial nature of what we call "intangible fixed assets" is not their significant characteristic from an accounting point of view. What is significant is the difficulty involved in measuring their value. There is, as intimated previously, a considerable variety of intangibles, and none of them can be approached on an assumption of permanence —as can, for example, land. Some intangibles have a prescribed term and others an indefinite term; some represent precisely defined rights and others rather vague advantages. Of this wide variety of intangibles, some of the more common types deserve at least brief consideration.

Patents

To come to grips with the variety in intangibles, let us first consider patent rights—a type of asset which provides an instructive field for study. Patent rights are granted for precise, specified terms; and as long as the cost basis of accounting is accepted, it is easy to persuade one's self that there is no problem in valuing patents. For example, the cost of a patent can be written off over its stipulated life just as neatly as can a prepaid insurance premium. But we should at once emphasize one very important difference between writing off the cost of a patent and writing off a prepaid insurance premium. In the case of the insurance premium, the cost is a good indication of value. There may be rate increases which make the value of the unexpired premium somewhat higher than cost; and the reverse will hold true if rates fall. However, under normal circumstances, such changes come gradually; and, as prepaid premiums are usually for three-year policies, it would be in very exceptional cases that the unamortized cost of the premium was not a good indication of its current value. For patents, it is quite a different matter. For one thing, patents run for a much longer period; and even though cost may be a good indication of value at the time that the patent is taken out, very large variations may occur—thus making the cost either far too high or much too low. Moreover, the value of a patent may bear little relation to its cost, even at the time at which the patent is taken out. In short, a proper concept of value is difficult in the patent field. Even if a reasonable value has been established by some sort of study, a new invention might unexpectedly wipe out such value overnight.

Thus, even for patent rights, which have a clearly specified term, the amortization of cost is not a satisfactory basis of valuation. The situation is further confused by the difficulty involved in determining what the cost of a patent is. If a patent is purchased in an arm's length transaction, there is some indication of market value. The trouble is that many patents are developed by the companies who use them and are therefore not purchased from other sources. In such cases, the cost of the patent gets buried in the operating expenses of the company. If there is a well-organized research department, then research expenses may be separately accumulated and may subsequently be written off, or carried forward, on some methodical basis. But it must be very rare that the research costs involved in developing a given patent can be isolated so as to provide a realistic cost for a specific patent. It follows that accountants usually treat purchased patents quite differently from patents that have been developed by a company for its own use. The cost of the purchased patent is set up as an asset; the developed patent is not. But this is nonsense! Someone who is buying or selling the company's shares is just as interested in one type as in the other.

Naturally, as patents can be valuable assets, it would be desirable to include their value along with that of other assets. But can they be realistically valued? In some instances, undoubtedly, a realistic value can be ascertained. There may be an offer from someone who wishes to buy the patent; or similar patents may recently have changed hands at a fair price; or the owner of the patent may license others to use it, and some useful value may be calculated from the royalty earnings. While in the cases mentioned, some valuation that is useful for accounting could be established, there are many instances where a basis for valuation simply does not exist. We must reluctantly conclude that (at least at the current stage of development of the accounting art) in many instances, and perhaps in most instances, the value of patent rights cannot be satisfactorily measured.

Accountants are thus left with a choice of two alternatives: either they can measure the value of patents where they are able to, and ignore such values where they cannot; or they can leave patent values out of the reckoning entirely. Accountants have tended to prefer the former course;

I prefer the latter. In my opinion, where there are insoluble difficulties in the measurement of a certain type of asset in a majority of the instances in which it is encountered, it is less confusing to ignore this type of asset entirely. If we do so, then anyone who reads a financial statement may safely assume that the statement does not purport to include such values. This is the sort of question which requires much more research than it has had so far, and it is the sort of question which should be dealt with in our code of ground rules. In the changing world in which we live, any code of rules will need constant improvement if it is intended to meet new problems and to take advantage of new analytical possibilities. It is possible that some day a reasonably reliable method of measuring patent values will be developed. And if this happens, we will then be able to produce better financial statements. For the time being, I recommend that we expense the cost of patents. This does not mean that patents should be ignored entirely, since it may well be that some useful information could be included in notes to statements. My feeling is only that patent values should not be included on the asset side of the balance sheet.

Other Intangibles

Patents have been selected as an illustration of the problems involved in valuing the so-called intangibles because they represent about the most clear-cut type of asset in this category. When we come to brand names and other goodwill items, valuation is even more difficult. For one thing, there is seldom a clear-cut expiry date, and there is therefore no way of establishing useful life. In addition to this, there are all the problems which make valuation so difficult in the case of patents.

Individual intangibles are thus exceedingly difficult to value. It is possible to approach the valuation of all intangibles taken together—or, to put the matter more generally, of all the assets which a company owns and which are not measurable. This can be done, at least after a fashion, by plotting the past earnings of the company in comparison with an agreed normal rate of earnings. Establishing "normal" rates presents problems, but stock market averages and similar statistics can provide some indication of normality. This can never be anything but arbitrary, but it can perhaps provide a useful rough guide. Granting all the difficulties, and the room for argument in selecting suitable comparisons, investors have always been able, nevertheless, to settle on rates which they consider "normal." By capitalizing earnings in excess of such arbitrary norms, a valuation (of sorts) for the intangibles may be reached.

I do not suggest that this is a procedure which would produce a value satisfactory for accounting purposes. It is simply a suggested approach to tackling a virtually insoluble problem.

It can readily be seen that the valuation of intangibles is nebulous to a high degree. Is any attempt at valuation so arbitrary, and so far from solid criteria, that the whole operation is not worth doing? Or, on the other hand, is there some value in such calculations—even granting all its inadequacies? This is the kind of question which needs further exploration. For my part, I have already stated my preference—which is to leave out the intangibles entirely in the present state of the art.

Deferred Costs

Amidst the intangibles in the modern balance sheet may be found various types of deferred cost. On the "allocation of cost" principle on which we now operate, there is merit in carrying forward some expenditures which are expected to benefit future periods—for example, the cost of special advertising campaigns, or research work on products that will sell in later years. To the extent that there is a genuine creation of values which will bear fruit in future years, there is logic in deferment. However, since the values created in both advertising campaigns and research are apt to be highly problematical, it seems to me that it would be less confusing if such deferrals were made only in cases in which it could reasonably be demonstrated that values had been created from which there were strong expectations of future benefits. Even when some assets were included to recognize the anticipated benefits to future years, it would be more logical to estimate such value—rather than just to carry forward cost.

To someone who thinks like an accountant, there is something soothing and reassuring about a systematic allocation of unusual costs over a period of years. But for reasons mentioned throughout this text, there is little support for such spreading out of costs in logic. I am inclined to believe that for an investor, or for any other statement-user, such amortizations simply confuse the issue. Where a reasonable estimate of value is not possible, I would rather see the expenditure expensed— with, perhaps, the addition of descriptive notes to explain what had been done and to point out that future benefits were expected.

Market versus Accounting Value

There is one other approach to the valuation of intangibles which is worth some consideration. This method consists of comparing the book value of the company (as shown by its balance sheet) with the value that would result from taking the latest market quotation for its shares and multiplying this by the number of shares outstanding. The difference between these two figures is the measure of the value which investors, in general, place on the unrecorded assets of the company. Under present accounting principles, this is not perhaps a very meaningful figure—the reason being that the difference between the quoted market value of a share and its book value now includes not only the investor's valuation of unrecorded assets, but also the various understatements of asset value which accounting principles (now generally accepted) permit. However, if a current-value basis were accepted for all other assets, the difference between market value and book value would represent precisely the value which the market places on the unrecorded intangibles.

To say the least, a comparison between market quotation and book value per share is an extremely interesting figure in statement analysis. It establishes how much the investor is paying for values in excess of those disclosed in the balance sheet—and in some cases, this figure will prove a significant and startling bit of information for the investor. However, although this approach to valuation of intangibles is of some interest, it is not a very satisfactory approach from the point of view of accounting theory. Accounting theory should be designed to produce financial statements which aid the investor in calculating a reasonable price for the shares which he intends to purchase. These statements should help him as much as possible, and the accountant who prepares the statements has the duty of giving as adequate data as possible for an investment decision. It is, therefore, the accountant who should be charged with producing a valuation—rather than leaving him to surmise what the value is by the price which investors are actually prepared to pay. For the investor to reach a decision on the value of the company by some sort of intuitive insight, and then for the accountant to use the investor's assessment in preparing his own assessment of asset values is exactly the wrong way about.

This discussion of intangibles is intended to throw some light on the whole difficult problem of asset valuation, since asset valuation represents one of the extremely difficult and tricky areas in accounting. It is hoped that this review of some of the complexities will be informative. However, to someone who wants to produce a better statement right now, complexities are of relatively little use. What he needs is a sensible working solution. In view of all the difficulties inherent in intangible-asset valuation, I believe that all that should be attempted at this stage is to give, in notes to the statements, as much descriptive data as possible regarding these assets.

At the same time, the valuation of intangible assets is a field in which a great deal of work can usefully be done on measurement techniques, and it is hoped that new procedures will be developed which make it possible to record, in some reasonably intelligent way, the current values of at least some intangible assets. We must remember, in attempting to reform financial statements, that we should not wait for cataclysmic new insights which will wash away all our problems. If better statements are to be produced, it will be by means of a long, gradual, and experimental process. Even if, for the time being, intangible assets have to be left out of financial statements entirely, it would at least be a great step forward to clear up other unsatisfactory areas in the measurement of current and fixed assets. And it would be less confusing to leave intangibles out entirely than to include them on the partial hit-and-miss basis which is now in effect.

What we set out to do in preparing financial statements is to measure assets which are reasonably measurable. However, the area in which measurement is possible can be expected to change with the development of new techniques. To take the convenient (and spectacular) example of computers: their introduction has made possible much more accurate measurements in many areas. For example, working out revaluations of complicated holdings of machinery becomes much more feasible if computer records of machinery have been maintained. Today, complicated plants may be revalued where previously it would not have been possible to recalculate values within the strict time limits necessarily imposed in financial reporting. A set of financial statements must come out very promptly if it is to be of any practical use. As a result, it is common for statements to be published, by even the largest and most complicated corporations, within six weeks of the close of a financial year. Speedy calculations on computers open up new possibilities for the satisfactory measurement of asset values in many directions.

As an example of how computers assist in the valuation process, let us consider the accounts receivable of a corporation which has a vast number of customers. It is generally accepted accounting practice that receivables should be stated at their face value less some provision for accounts which are expected to be slow or to turn bad. For many years, it was considered a satisfactory way of calculating the provision for bad and doubtful accounts to proceed by a process that accountants describe as "aging." This process involved an analysis of the accounts to show

how long they had been owing. Accounts were sorted into several categories: thirty days old, ninety days old, six months old, overdue beyond a year—or into some such classification. Then, by a simple process of analysis, the average age of the accounts could be struck and a provision for doubtful accounts calculated on some simple formula—such as 25 percent of the accounts over three months, 50 percent over six months, and 100 percent over one year—or something of this sort. For companies where there were too many accounts to make it feasible to analyse all of them (which is, in fact, the typical case), samples were selected and a percentage established which was then assumed to hold for all the receivables. While most of this work was of a very rough-and-ready nature, it was really as far as it was practical to go prior to the invention of the computer.

While the technique of aging had to be relied upon when there was no possibility of making a more searching scrutiny of the receivables, the accountant would have naturally preferred to examine each account to observe the pattern of transactions—and ideally, the best valuation of receivables would probably result from an individual scrutiny and assessment of each account. With the aid of a computer, a much closer approach to this ideal is now sometimes possible. A computer may at least be programmed to draw out accounts that might require special scrutiny—for example, accounts where the pattern of purchases has altered in a significant manner, or where credit notes are frequent, or where non-cash credits have occurred, and so on. This practice might improve the valuation which is possible under the rough-and-ready approach of aging.

CHAPTER 13

Other Assets and Liabilities

We have gone, in some depth, into the problems of valuing different types of assets. For the most part, these assets have been ones which are important and which, by their nature, provide an interesting illustration of the complexities involved in the process of valuation. It is to be hoped that in exploring these problems we have established the general principle that all such difficulties can be dealt with so long as we concentrate on the basic purpose of financial reporting—which is, to provide statements which are useful to those who need financial information. In the process of valuation, many different techniques are appropriate in different circumstances, and I have tried to establish that this variety in techniques is not anything to worry about so long as, in each case, we use an appropriate technique to produce a realistic approximation to current value. To complete our consideration of the asset side of the balance sheet, it is perhaps worth making brief mention of a few other types of assets.

Cash

No special problem would seem to be involved in valuing cash, since valuation is simply the process of converting non-cash assets to cash. In some cases, there are restrictions on the use of cash, but here the only requirement is that we indicate such restrictions where they are judged to be significant. One also encounters currency in foreign exchange, but the accepted and sensible method of handling this problem is to convert the foreign exchange balances at current rates.

Marketable Securities

Where there is a ready market for shares, there should normally be few valuation problems. Special situations, however, can present difficulties. The normal market for the shares of a corporation is for what are called "board lots"—and this implies relatively small transactions. But if a very large number of shares are held (in proportion to the total shares outstanding) the market quotations may not provide a reliable value. It is dangerous to assume that large holdings can be liquidated at approximately-current quotation levels, since the sale of a substantial holding will sometimes drive the market price down appreciably.

On the other hand, a holding that is sufficient to give control of the company may be worth more than the market quote. In valuing securities which are held as a temporary investment of surplus funds, this problem of large holding is not likely to be encountered. But it may be; and the present discussion is intended to emphasize the fact that valuations, if they are to be right, must be done intelligently and not just by blindly following established rules. If a situation is encountered where, say, there is a very large holding of securities, but less than a controlling interest, the accountant must decide whether or not it is realistic to use market quotations in valuing the shares. There is no pat answer, and the proper decision will depend on circumstances. It is to some extent comforting to reflect that full disclosure of what is decided upon is at least a partial justification of any treatment adopted.

Shares of Subsidiary Companies

Where a controlling interest is held in a corporation, the market quotation could be very misleading, because the purchase of control of a corporation is a transaction quite different from purchasing a share in the minority interest.

There are two recognized methods of stating the value of shares in subsidiary companies. Such shares may be carried at cost, or they may be carried at cost adjusted by increases or decreases in book value since date of acquisition. The latter method comes very close to approximating a current-value approach, and I therefore much prefer it. If the accounts of the subsidiary were on a current-value basis, the situation would be even more satisfactory. The valuation of the subsidiary company shares arises only when consolidated statements are not produced. As the current vogue is for consolidated statements to be issued in all but exceptional cases, not too large a problem should be encountered under this heading.

Other Non-Marketable Securities

Frequently, a company holds an important investment in shares for which there is no market. When a controlling interest is not held, the usually accepted procedure is to carry such shares at cost. This is very likely to be an unsatisfactory value, but it is difficult to suggest a satisfactory alternative.

Where a controlling interest is not held, it is not customary to use the technique (mentioned above in regard to shares of subsidiary companies) of adjusting the value of the holdings by profits and losses subsequent to acquisition. It is not too clear why this procedure is sanctioned for majority holdings but not for minority interests. The reason is perhaps to be found in the notion that control of a company permits a parent company to decide such matters as dividend distributions. But this is not a very good reason for sanctioning a type of valuation in one case and not in another.

A large investment in a non-marketable corporation is likely to be for some special purpose, and it is possible that a fair method of valuation will be suggested by the special circumstances of the case. Where no better valuation basis suggests itself, the best treatment might be to adopt the method already sanctioned for holding companies—i.e., to carry the shares at original cost adjusted to reflect change in equity since acquisition. It is interesting to observe that the Accounting and Auditing Research Committee of the CICA has now suggested that this treatment might be appropriate.[13]

However difficult this problem may be, it is most unlikely that original cost will be the most informative presentation, unless the purchase of shares is a recent one and there has been little change in circumstances since acquisition.

Unmeasurable Assets

As has already been intimated, there are many kinds of assets—and, in fact, very genuine assets—which the accountant makes no attempt to

---

13. *Handbook of The Canadian Institute of Chartered Accountants*, Section 3014.10.

value. An outstanding example of this is the human values which every corporation possesses. These assets range all the way from the special contribution of exceptional leaders down to a good supply of general workers. It is, of course, a very real advantage to a company to be strong in these respects. But the question is: can such advantage be measured in any realistic way? In other words—is there any way of placing a value on such assets which will mean anything to anybody?

There are some rather intriguing possibilities. Let us first do a casual exercise in a rather specialized field—a field where valuing human assets might not be too tough. In the somewhat unusual circumstances presented by a baseball club, for example, could a system be established to produce a reasonable accounting for the value of its players? Baseball is a field which I know only through the pages of the daily newspapers; but even on the basis of this limited acquaintance, a few things seem to me to be clearly evident. In the first place, it is obvious that baseball is a pastime which is absolutely riddled with statistics. One need only listen to the voice on television on any afternoon: "Harry McGraw has just told me that when Leo Manuelo hit a foul tip in the second inning, he tied a record held by 18 other pitchers in the American League for hitting a foul tip on two successive appearances at the plate against a right-handed pitcher with the count at 1-0." Where there is this wealth of statistics available, accounting measurement holds unlimited possibilities.

I gather from the sports pages that it is quite common for baseball clubs to give enormous bonuses to callow high-school youths for simply signing a contract. From the statistics of the past, it should not be too difficult to make a reasonable estimate of how likely it is that such "bonus babies" will succeed: how many years they are likely to spend in the minors; how many years as a starting pitcher; how many years in relief; and, finally, how many years back in the minors. From all this, it should be possible to calculate the useful life of a baseball pitcher, just as it is possible to calculate the useful life of ordinary types of machinery— a task which we regard as a matter of routine. By extending our efforts, it might not be too difficult to reach a valuation for a group of baseball players which would bear some relation to reality. We would then be in a position, at least, to do as sensible an accounting for human values as we now accomplish for various types of fixed assets.

More scientific approaches are brewing in this field. The Institute for Social Research of the University of Michigan has engaged in serious studies of what is described as "accounting for human resources." As a paper prepared by one of the researchers says: "Financial planning and control practices and accounting measurements are recognized as critical for the successful operation of a large organization. Yet accountants continue to ignore one of the most important resources of an organization—its people." Starting from this premise, research studies have already been undertaken in an effort to find the extent to which it is possible to produce a practical and useful accounting for the human resources of a company.

This project is of the greatest possible importance. At present, companies are spending increasing amounts of both time and money on recruiting and training programs for all levels of staff. In this way, they are spending money unproductively now, in the hope that later periods will benefit. They are continually having to decide how much should be spent in this manner, and, at the moment, most companies operate more or less in the dark. This is not a satisfactory situation. It is impossible for management decisions to be made intelligently unless some estimate can be made of the effectiveness of training and development programs.

Surely it would be useful for a company to know whether its human resources are being increased, maintained, or run down. In what other way can a company know whether or not it is using its resources effectively? How much better off is a company as a result of its training programs? Should it spend more on them? In the research which will ultimately provide answers to these questions, a start has been made on the human resources within the company. But, as researchers point out, there are also valuable human resources outside the company. Good relations with customers, distributors, suppliers, and shareholders can all be important to the success of a company; and a good deal of money is spent by most companies in developing good relations with these groups. If an accounting for human resources could be developed, companies would for the first time be in a position to estimate how various projects of promoting good public relations are turning out—that is to say, how much value has been created by the money spent.

It may be observed that here again the important thing is to achieve some notion of the current value of this part of a company's assets. And to the extent that this can be approached, more sensible decisions can be made. We are a long way from setting up asset values which represent reliably the value of personnel, or the value of good external relationships. It is, nevertheless, encouraging that the importance of this kind of subject is appreciated by someone, and that a serious attack is being mounted on the problems which are likely to be encountered. Here again is a clear example of a field where there is more than ample room for scientific research.

Liabilities

Having valued the advantages which a company has, we must be equally careful to reach a realistic value of its obligations. The most important figure in any set of financial statements is the amount of net assets, and both sides of the balance sheet must be stated realistically if this key figure is to be correct. Thus, the finest work of asset valuation is wasted unless equal attention is given to the task of determining the actual economic liabilities of the company. And with liabilities, just as with assets, we are certain to encounter every kind of problem—from simple, clear-cut liabilities (which it is easy to state properly) all the way to vague and indefinite liabilities (to which it is much harder to attach a definite figure).

Accounting started out with a strong legalistic bias. The notion was that a liability need only be acknowledged when it represented an actual legal claim against the company. Today, however, this is clearly an inadequate concept. The essential purpose of the balance sheet is to portray the favourable and unfavourable factors in a company's financial position, and, by deducting the latter from the former, to reach a net value which has some significance. Clearly, it would be unsatisfactory to value the asset side of the balance sheet on the basis of economics and the liability side on the basis of legal claims.

The criterion for recognizing a liability must simply be that it is an unfavourable factor—i.e., something that will have to be paid in future, or is likely to have to be paid, or is likely to diminish future revenue. To illustrate this, we might consider several types of problem in accounting for liabilities:

1) Term

In order for the current liquid position of a company to be apparent, its liabilities must be segregated into those which are due currently and those which are due some years hence. This presents no insuperable difficulties. The present convention holds that any liability which is expected to mature within a year should be considered current, and that any liability which is expected to mature later than a year should be considered long-term. This convention seems sensible enough, and there is therefore little reason to alter it.

2) *Measurement*

There are some cases which are very difficult to measure. For example, a court case against a company may involve a potential liability of considerable dimensions. But as to how likely it is that the liability will materialize depends on the outcome of the case; and in the meantime, one must rely largely on the opinion of management or its legal counsel.

There would be no law case if everyone could foresee the outcome. When a case is being fought, it is only human for each side to persuade itself that it is going to win. It is thus particularly difficult to place a figure on the estimated amount of the final settlement.

As it is unlikely that large corporations with far-flung operations will be able to avoid becoming involved in lawsuits, it may be taken for granted that any corporation, at each balance-sheet date, will have a number of cases in progress. It is therefore only necessary to draw attention to either very large or extraordinary cases. This limits the problem somewhat. For the big cases, about all that the accountant can do is to disclose the possibility of a claim in a footnote. This is most unsatisfactory—particularly in view of the fact that the corporation is always understandably anxious (so as not to prejudice its case) to admit as little concern as possible about the outcome. But how else can the situation be handled? More research please!

Insurance companies understand this problem very well—as frequently one of their most important liabilities is for claims which are in the process of being settled. Insurance companies have, however, a wealth of experience in these matters; and, relying on the law of averages, they can usually reach some reasonable estimate of their total liability.

3) *"Going concern" values*

There are certain payments which a company is not obliged to make legally, but which it must make if it is to continue to operate as a successful corporation. A good example of this is non-contractual pension payments.

These payments arise from the fact that every firm must retain good staff. Its trained staff is an important asset to it, and such staff will not remain with the company unless they expect to be reasonably treated—and it would naturally disturb them if they observed that the company did not treat its staff properly at retirement. Even with the funded pension plans which now exist in most companies, there is always the likelihood that some employees will reach retirement without having built up adequate pensions. In such cases, it is common for the company to make *ex gratia* payments in order to bring their pensions up to what it considers a more appropriate level. While these payments are not obligatory in the legal sense of the word, it is nevertheless necessary for the company to make them—for if it failed to do so, the effect on staff morale could be disastrous.

When anyone purchases a company outright, the liability for these unfunded pensions is almost always investigated. It is usually possible to make some sort of quasi-actuarial calculation. Clearly, this liability can be very important in the purchase of a business; and, as previously indicated in another context, if this is significant when a business is purchased, then, by the same token, it is important whenever the company issues financial statements.

The answer seems clear enough. The liability for unfunded pensions should be estimated and set up every time that a balance sheet is prepared.

4) *The time element*

The time at which a liability must be met is clearly relevant. The whole theory on which our economy is based is centered about the idea that money has value. If you hold a sum of money for a certain period, the interest which you pay reflects the fact that you have enjoyed this value for that period of time. With liabilities, however, the reverse is true. It is less onerous to pay a liability a year hence than to pay it currently, because you have the use of the money in the meantime. It is therefore illogical to record a debt of $100 which is due one year hence at the same figure as a debt of $100 which must be paid immediately.

In the case of bond issues, the time factor is automatically taken into consideration. We record the ultimate redemption price of the bond at full value only because we pay interest on this amount until maturity. In this case, it is correct to record the full face value, because, through the obligation to pay interest in the intervening time, the obligation to redeem the bond is just as onerous as a current payment of the same amount.

Our accounting for bonds payable would in fact be better (i.e., more accurate) if we were to adjust the amount of the liability in accordance with changes in the going rate of interest. For example, a bond issue which is made before interest rates rise can be an important advantage to a company, and this should be reflected in the company's financial statements. Similarly, of course, bonds which are issued before interest rates fall are an onerous liability. It would be fairly easy to work out a calculation to adjust the liability each time by applying the going rate of interest.

Long-term liabilities where no interest is payable are perhaps not particularly common. But where they are encountered, it would seem only sensible that the same principle apply. This means that such liabilities should be discounted to produce a present value, using the current effective interest rate. There can be difference of opinion as to what rate to use, but it should not be impossible to select a reasonably appropriate rate—which would be better than ignoring the time factor entirely.

If the time factor is consistently applied to all liabilities, there will no doubt be many complications. However, in the normal case at least, long-term liabilities, while they may be large, are not numerous—and perhaps a calculation of the time factor would not prove particularly difficult. As far as current liabilities are concerned, it is unlikely that the time factor will be material. Moreover, there is often a natural offset between receivables and payables—an offset which would mean that the net difference was not material and could therefore be ignored. In any event, the matter is clear enough in common sense and in logic. And until somebody demonstrates that to calculate present values of liabilities consistently would prove a tremendously difficult task, it would seem reasonable to advocate that we do so.

What is said of liabilities, of course, applies also to assets. There are many anomalies in balance-sheet presentation which are created by the fact that accountants ignore the factor of time. For example, it is not uncommon to write buildings off over a period of forty or fifty years on the straight-line method of depreciation. But, ignoring the time factor over a period of this duration is completely unrealistic, and the results obtained by straight-line depreciation over long periods cannot possibly be proper.

5) *Foreign exchange*

Accounting for foreign exchange raises another interesting point. Conventional accounting has a highly developed system for applying different foreign exchange rates to different types of assets and liabilities. The spot rate of exchange is used for current assets and liabilities—naturally enough. For fixed assets, however, and for the corresponding accumulation of depreciation, it is customary to use the rate of foreign exchange which applied at the date of acquisition of the asset. This is perfectly sensible as long as we adhere to the cost basis of valuation. However, as that basis is illogical, the practice leads to silly results.

For example, a building that was purchased in England for a certain sum in pounds sterling may have to appear in the balance sheet of a Canadian corporation in terms of Canadian dollars. Surely, if sterling deteriorates in terms of Canadian dollars, it is unrealistic to continue to convert the asset for purposes of inclusion in the Canadian-dollar statement at the old rate of exchange. If an asset is bought in sterling, and if sterling drops, then surely some loss has been sustained. And the reverse is true if sterling rises.

Unless current rates of exchange are used throughout the entire financial statement, very serious anomalies are bound to appear. Let us take the case of a Canadian company which issues bonds payable forty years hence in U.S. funds. (It is quite common for Canadian corporations and governments to do this in order to gain access to the U.S. bond market.) At present, the Canadian dollar is at a discount of 8 percent in terms of American dollars. Thus, if one million dollars worth of bonds are issued at par in U.S. funds, the company will receive $1,080,000 in Canadian funds. So far as I know, there is no recognized rule to guide the company as to how this transactions should be recorded in its financial statements—and needless to say, it presents quite a problem.

Consider the possibilities. Firstly, the $80,000 can be treated as a premium and amortized over the life of the bonds in the way that is normally applicable to bond premiums. However, the $80,000 is not like ordinary bond premium which arises when a $100 bond is issued at a premium, in local currency, through market factors. In this latter situation, the premium automatically disappears at redemption date, and it makes perfectly good sense to amortize it systematically over the life of the bond. But when a Canadian company issues securities repayable in U.S. dollars, the premium will disappear at redemption date only if Canadian and American currencies have moved to par by that time. And there is no more reason to expect that this will happen than to assume a further decline in the rate against Canada.

Because both the United States and Canada call their currencies "dollars," the idea seems to circulate that it is normal for these currencies to be at par. This is not an assumption which anyone would make when considering, say, French francs and Japanese yen; and yet it would be just as logical to assume that the rate between these two currencies should normally be at par. In short, it is quite illogical to look at par as being the normal rate of exchange. It was indeed so in the relatively brief period when the gold standard worked properly. But under present conditions, I can see nothing to be said for the reasonableness of assuming that the Canadian and American dollars are likely to be at par at some future date. Going back to our illustration, it would therefore be incorrect for the Canadian company which issued U.S. dollar pay bonds to amortize the premium in the customary way.

Another possibility is that the $80,000 exchange premium be retained on the books as a liability until the maturity of the bond issue. However, in this case, we are assuming that the 8 percent discount rate will still obtain when the bonds reach redemption date; and once again we are making an assumption which we have no reason to make. The fact is that over the past forty years, Canadian dollars, in terms of United States dollars, have varied from a discount of approximately 30 percent to a premium of approximately 10 percent. The exchange rate has been at par from time to time, but not with a consistency which would make this seem the habitual situation. There is simply no logical way of predicting what the exchange rate will be forty years hence. Consequently, the only reasonable procedure is to carry the liability for the bond issue at current rates of exchange. As the exchange rate rises or falls, it is reasonable and sensible to adjust the liability to take up the profit or loss which has, in effect, occurred. Moreover, as a practical matter, it is much less likely that violent fluctuations will suddenly occur in the accounts. It is possible for an exchange rate to change suddenly and drastically, but it is more likely that a significant variation will take place over a long period of years. It does not make sense to ignore current fluctuations throughout the entire life of the bonds, and to then face a sudden adjustment, quite unrelated to any economic occurrence, when the bond becomes due.

We must once again remember that what we are producing is periodic financial statements, and that our aim should be to show what the position is during the period covered by the statement. In our example of the bond issue, if the money is borrowed when the Canadian dollar is at a discount of 8 percent, and if at the end of the next year the rate moves to a discount of 4 percent, the company is obviously better off by $40,000 owing to developments during the period for which the accounting is being made. By incurring a liability of $1,000,000 U.S. funds, it has got $40,000 more Canadian than would a competitor who borrowed a year later.

6) *Leases*

Long-term leases present all sorts of problems in accounting—many of which we have not really properly coped with yet. Take, for example, the case of a simple long-term lease at a fixed rental. If rents rise, this lease represents an asset which should surely be reflected in the company's financial statements. And by the same token, if rents fall, the same lease is clearly a liability. There is no problem of setting up the asset or liability which this creates, except for the problem of finding comparable rents so that changes in level can be determined—and normally, this should not present a particularly difficult computation.

Nowadays, of course, very few long-term leases are for fixed rentals. If there is an escalation clause in the lease (and this is likely to be the case), there may not be any need to consider the problem of asset or liability. If the rent is to move with ordinary price-level changes, no particular gain or loss is implied.

A simple straightforward lease is, alas, somewhat unusual. There are apt to be repurchase commitments which can make the situation quite complex. The basic principle to adhere to is that if a long-term lease is entered into, and if a change in market conditions makes the lease more or less favourable than it was when issued, then some kind of asset or liability has materialized—and it should be within the bounds of human ingenuity to figure some way of measuring this in a satisfactory way.

Theory and Practice

There are many other special situations, but we have perhaps gone far enough in the discussion of liabilities to show what a jungle it presents. Some of the suggestions made, such as the discounting of assets and liabilities in recognition of the time factor, will be thought radical. I have heard good accountants say that this is a preposterously impractical idea. Well, so it may turn out to be. I have little confidence, however, in opinions which are given with assurance, but without any experience of what difficulties will actually be encountered.

If there is any merit at all in trying to produce useful statements, the idea of taking cognizance of the time factor would seem to be absolutely sound. If, after serious attempts to put this into effect, it turns out that insuperable difficulties are encountered, then the idea will have to be abandoned—and we will then recognize this as a refinement which it is simply not practical to introduce. Similarly with the suggestions about leases.

From what limited experimentation I have seen seriously undertaken, it is my impression that great improvements could be immediately introduced. And it is also my impression that these improvements could be achieved without encountering difficulties which could not be solved sufficiently to make the resulting statements better than those which we have now. This, in fact, is the whole burden of my song.

Materiality

This is perhaps a good place to refer briefly to the question of materiality. "Materiality," in accounting, is a matter of fundamental importance. Whatever logical reasons there may be for this or that accounting treatment, if anything but genuinely significant amounts are involved, it cannot matter which treatment is adopted.

This is another of those subjects to which accountants pay lip service readily enough, but which they tend to waver on in practice. For example, in the event of a gross violation of accounting propriety, accountants are likely to take issue even if the amounts involved are less than significant—as, for example, when the two sides of the balance sheet are out of agreement by some trivial amount owing to sloppy bookkeeping.

Thus, you will find accountants who argue seriously that materiality is not entirely a quantitative matter. With this contention, however, I strongly disagree. Unless the amount at issue is so large that correcting it would be likely to change the opinion of a statement-user, there can be no reason for making the correction. If this view were consistently maintained, we would be more inclined to focus our attention on the important implications of statements—instead of allowing ourselves to be absorbed in fussy and inconsequential issues.

This point is stressed here because many of the difficulties which are likely to be involved in producing current-value statements would appear much less formidable if we were to remain strictly faithful to our materiality concept and to seek only those adjustments of cost which are genuinely significant. A good example of this is the discounting of liabilities to current value—a task which would be enormous if undertaken meticulously, but which might be quite manageable if we confined ourselves to material items.

CHAPTER 14

The Income Statement

Up to this point in our discussion, we have devoted more attention to the balance sheet than we have to the income statement. The balance sheet has been given this greater emphasis, not because it is more important than the income statement, but because it seems to provide a better approach to the subject for purposes of exposition. As the balance sheet and income statement are completely articulated, it follows that any adjustment to the one will also affect the other. If we accept the idea that value is the important thing in accounting, then it almost inevitably follows that the balance sheet is the correct approach to the income statement—rather than the other way around.

It is surprising how many people seem to assume that the balance sheet is an out-of-date statement. They feel that net income is the most important figure, and they seem to believe, contrary to logic, that you can have a realistic figure for net income without necessarily having realistic balance-sheet values. This is absurd. Balance-sheet values get amortized through the income account, and if the values are not realistic values, then the resulting net-income figure is not realistic either. To my mind, it makes no sense to maintain that a certain net income has been earned unless it can be demonstrated that net assets have been increased by that amount. If a certain income is earned, then the net worth of the company must increase by that amount—and if you follow this back logically, you are forced to conclude that since balance-sheet values result from an accumulation of income figures, either both statements are realistically stated or neither is.

As has been pointed out earlier, there are two stages by which better values can be introduced into financial statements: the first step is to give some indication of the value of assets and liabilities by way of footnotes; and the second step is to incorporate such current values into the body of the balance sheet. The result of this second step is that income is adjusted to a current-value basis also—whereas if current values are simply mentioned in notes to the financial statements, the income figure is left unadjusted. From this point of view, the incorporating of current values into the actual statements is far preferable to merely providing information in footnotes.

As far as the income account goes, the overwhelmingly important figure is the final net income from transactions and from valuation adjustments. The net income so established can be analysed and presented in a variety of forms. However, there is not much hope of reaching a standardized form of income presentation that will prove satisfactory to all companies, since the operations of different companies vary widely and the form of presentation will depend on the type of operation being reported on. Nevertheless, a few general rules may be suggested—though generalizations do not carry very far in the income statement. There are simply too many basically different kinds of operation to deal with.

A standardized classification of revenues and expenditures within an industry is desirable, since standardization means that comparisons between companies can more readily be made. But even here, with the trend towards diversity of lines (as exemplified by the emergence of "conglomerates"), it is often difficult to find truly relevant comparisons. There remains some merit in standard forms of presentation for such broad categories as railways, public utilities, and retail stores.

Revenue

Gross volume is important and useful information for investors. Many basic analytic ratios are built on gross revenue. In large corporations with diversified products, total gross revenue may not be a really significant figure, unless analysed by product line. Non-recurring or extraordinary revenue should be shown separately.

Expenditure

There has never been a settled consensus on the best approach to classifying expenditure for statement purposes. Here again, the nature of the operation may be the decisive consideration, and standard treatments may prove quite inappropriate for different types of enterprise.

Even for manufacturing companies (the classical type of concern for illustrative purposes in accounting texts), at least two different concepts have gained support. The traditional approach to classification of expenditure is based on an attempt to parallel the production-sales process. Thus, the first classification is "cost of manufacture," following the production process. First, we enter the cost of the material and the direct labour which go into production, and we then add manufacturing overhead. The difference between "cost of manufacture" and "revenue" represents what is called "gross profit"—which is supposed to be what is "left over" to cover administration, selling expenses, and income tax, and to provide a return to bondholders and owners in the form of interest and dividends.

This notion that manufacturing costs are somehow more real, or that they have primacy of importance because they come first (you have to make something before you can sell it), is now often questioned. Selling and administrative expenses are as essential to the whole process as manufacturing expenses. This being the case, it can be argued that the classical concept of gross profit is misleading. It would be just as logical to start out by deducting administration expenses from revenue—thus producing a balance available for manufacturing expenses, selling expenses, and profit. Or you could start out by deducting budgeted profit from gross revenue and thus establish the amount available for expenditure—and this approach, in fact, appeals to me as a cost-control concept.

Following this line of thought, we might note that the single-step form of income statement achieved some popularity. Under this concept, the accountant uses broad categories of expense such as material costs, personnel costs, taxes, supplies, etc.—the total of all these categories being deducted from revenue to produce net income, with no intermediate subtotals to set forth profit before this, that, or the other thing.

The term "gross profit" was tending to disappear as a statement heading, on the grounds that it was misleading to use the term "profit" (however qualified) for a figure from which other expenses had to be deducted before any "profit" (in the normal sense of the word) could be claimed. However, just at that stage, the so-called "conglomerate" company began to attract the serious attention of investors—and therefore of government regulatory commissions. The conglomerate, as the name is supposed to imply, is an enterprise which deals in a wide variety of lines. Special attention has recently been focussed on the problems of proper accounting for such mixed enterprises, because the popular trend to diversification has made this type of operation much more common today.

The problem is that a single set of operating figures covering a wide variety of business undertakings is sometimes very hard to interpret. The first step towards improved disclosure was to require a breakdown of gross revenue into principal types of operation—sorting out heavy manufacturing from light, service revenue from product sales, commercial from financial income, and so on. The next step was to suggest that it would be more informative still if profit contribution could be similarly analysed. However, this step can present formidable difficulties at the net-income stage, as it might (in some cases at least) imply allocations of administrative expenses which would be so arbitrary as to be meaningless. The idea then emerged that it would perhaps be more practical to require profit contribution to be analysed at the gross-profit stage. Thus, interest is reviving in the gross-profit concept—a concept that is now more often called "gross margin."

Form and Content

I do not think that any further generalization on the form of the income statement would be useful at this stage. The crucial starting point is the acceptance of the net-income figure as basically measuring increase in value, after allowance for contributions and withdrawals and prior-year adjustments. Apart from the details of the form of statement, this leaves us with two important questions: (1) the distinction between holding and operating gains (or losses); and (2) the further distinction between normal and extraordinary operating gains (or losses).

Both of these matters have been touched upon in Chapter 5, and I have little to add to the question of how holding and operating figures should be reported. It seems to me that both types of gain must be disclosed, but I don't believe it matters much how this is done. I have a slight preference for keeping the cumulative gains separate in the equity section of the balance sheet; but the only essential requirement is that we show the amounts separately in the income statement. On the matter of normal and extraordinary operating gains, I think that the discussion in Chapter 5 should perhaps be carried a little further.

The "Normal" and the "Extraordinary"

We might remind ourselves once again that the results of past operations are useful only as a basis for projecting future profits. Thus, they should be presented in such a way as to facilitate projections—and this means distinguishing between what might be described as "normal" and "extraordinary" (or "abnormal") profits. The assumption is that normal profits are more likely to continue and are therefore a more reliable base for projections into the future. With this thought in mind, accountants have attempted to classify some types of profits and losses as "capital" rather than "revenue" items. For example, the sale of a factory will produce a profit or loss which cannot be considered as occurring in the ordinary course of business. The *idea* is all right; but this use of the terms "capital" and "revenue" is confusing, and, quite properly, is now discouraged. Similarly, losses due to a serious strike may be segregated, in the belief (perhaps an optimistic one) that they are abnormal and that this should be taken into account in estimating future-profit potential.

This special treatment of unusual items may frequently be useful to the investor, but one cannot help wondering whether the whole concept of "normal" items is not a little unrealistic. For instance, how abnormal is a strike these days? And as for the sale of fixed assets, disposals are often so frequent that they may be considered a normal part of the operations. For example, typewriters are usually classified as fixed assets having a life of from five to ten years. Thus, in theory at least, profit or loss on the sale of typewriters is a gain or loss on the sale of fixed assets. But the periodic replacement of typewriters may be so much a part of a large corporation's operations that the sale of typewriters is not really extraordinary at all. Indeed, large corporations which have substantial investments in equipment of this sort often adopt the policy of expensing such equipment immediately—on the grounds that expenditures on this type of asset are so normal an item, that there can be little distortion in profits as a result of charging the machines off to expense, even although they represent a considerable investment and are likely to be in use for a number of years.

Another illustration of the accountant's difficulties with the concept of normality is to be found in the conditions which prevailed during and after World War II. The outbreak of the war completely changed the operations of many of our most important corporations. Very heavy expenses were incurred in converting factories to war production, and further heavy expenditures were later incurred in converting them back to peacetime operation. An interesting argument developed as to whether these conversion expenses should be charged to wartime or to peacetime production—or, if apportioned, what share should go to each. As can be imagined, there was considerable support for the idea that peace is "normal" and that the conversion (both to wartime production and back to peacetime production) should therefore be charged to the war period. It has been pointed out, however, that this is logical only if we assume that peace is normal. And, looking back over the last century or so, it can be seen that for many Western countries, this is a rather dubious assumption. It is at least arguable that it is more realistic to consider war and peace as simply two alternating states—neither of which is any more "normal" than the other. This dismal but defensible view would suggest that conversion expenses should be allocated, by means of some formula, to *both* peacetime and wartime periods—rather than being loaded entirely on wartime production.

It is perhaps not surprising that accountants have wavered between insisting, on the one hand, on a clear distinction between the normal and the extraordinary and accepting resignedly, on the other, the fact that it is almost impossible to maintain such a distinction with consistent logic.

Gains on Disposal of Securities

In this connection, I inevitably think back to an early auditing experience in which our client was a small private manufacturing company which earned a net income in the neighbourhood of $100,000 a year. The company had been managed for a long time along extremely conservative lines, and had gradually accumulated a very large investment portfolio. It had been the company's practice, when securities were either purchased or sold, to bring the resulting profit or loss on the sale of securities directly to surplus. Inspired by the concept of the all-inclusive income account (a concept then in high fashion), we persuaded this client that these relatively minor profits and losses on security transactions should go through the income account. Now this was not a company which changed its accounting operations frequently or cheerfully, and by the time that it had been persuaded to come round to our point of view, a certain amount of heated argument had gone on.

As it turned out (by great misfortune, as I thought at the time), the very following year the company found and bought a tract of land on which to relocate its plant. This involved the liquidation of its large investment portfolio; and as this consisted of stocks purchased over a long period of time—stocks which had (quite properly, according to generally accepted accounting principles) been carried at cost—the result was an enormous profit on sale of securities which completely swamped the results of its manufacturing operations for the year. Those who have been through this kind of thing will appreciate the problems which faced us, at the next year end, when we had to persuade the client that the treatment which we had advocated with such earnestness the year before would now make nonsense of the income account, and that we should therefore revert to our former procedure. The proprietor of this business was a man of strong feelings, but, as it turned out, also fairminded. As a result, we were reappointed auditors for the following year.

It was a few traumatic experiences such as this which set me on my long and arduous journey towards something more defensible than the cost basis of accounting. Under current-value accounting, at least, absurd situations of this kind would be avoided. Profit or loss on investments would be recorded steadily, as it arose, and a company would never be faced with the necessity of taking up a large profit in a year in which none had occurred.

Other Problems

If we accept a change from cost to value accounting, we certainly create some new problems in reporting. For example, what do we do with the cherished distinction between realized and unrealized profits? In my view, we pitch it out entirely—on the grounds that it is a quite arbitrary rule of thumb which really has very little value. It is, moreover, replaced by the more useful distinction between holding and operating gains. Holding gains come from such things as changes in price level or in exchange rate, and there is in them an element of the external and the fortuitous—although this must not be pressed too far. A holding gain may represent shrewd purchasing, and shrewd purchasing is just as praiseworthy a quality and just as much a part of regular operations as any other management skill. Even when this is conceded, the analysis of profit between holding and operating results is informative.

To abandon, as I suggest we do, the distinction between realized and unrealized gains would require that some thought be given to the determination of profits available for dividends. This question used to absorb a great deal of the accountant's attention, and early legal cases often turned on this point. Some curious rulings resulted from the courts' attempt to distinguish between fixed and circulating capital; and these old cases are still treated with some reverence in accounting texts.

In the early days of the limited liability corporation (i.e., towards the middle of the last century), it was essential that attention be paid to the question of how much profit was distributable. While managers and shareholders were getting accustomed to this drastic new invention, the question of availability of dividends had to be stressed. Present-day balance sheets do not always show clearly what profits are available for dividends, and the reason for this is perhaps that, in North American practice at least, it is simply not a question which normally arises. The pattern that is virtually universal on this continent is for companies to retain a large portion of their earnings as one of the important methods of financing expansion. Under such circumstances, it is almost unheard of for a corporation of any standing to be short of available earnings for dividends. The normal situation is that the corporation has vast sums which are legally available for distribution but which it cannot distribute because the earnings have been reinvested in non-liquid assets. We can start confidently, then, with the assumption that the legal restriction on dividends, limiting them to the amount of profits realized, is not an effective way of ensuring a safe dividend policy.

Under value accounting, the balance-sheet values would at least be a better indication of the safe limits of dividend distribution than would our conventional statements. In either case, there is a liquidity problem as well as a problem of legal availability. Thus, whether we move to current-value accounting or not, it is high time that we developed accounting rules which deal more effectively with the problems of dividend payment.

In the details of the income statement there are interesting problems of disclosure and of presentation. But in my opinion, none of these are worth talking about until the essential step is taken of moving over to value-based accounting.

Intangibles

In our previous discussion of intangibles (see Chapter 12), it was suggested that our present treatment of such assets is intolerable. There are no very helpful rules for us to rely on in deciding whether some goodwill-type expenditures should be capitalized or expended; and once an intangible asset is set up, there are no rules to guide the accountant as to how the asset should be amortized. Under current-value accounting, these problems become problems of measurement. The fact that an asset is intangible does not mean that it should not be measured; but a good many of the so-called intangibles are, in fact, impossible to measure satisfactorily by the procedures which we have so far developed.

As you may recall, it was also suggested that in the current state of accounting, the best way to treat intangibles is to write them off—rather than attempt to capitalize them. At the same time, the hope was expressed that we would be able, at some point in the future, to develop measurement techniques which would prove sufficiently reliable to enable us to improve our statements by including intangibles.

If the proposal of expensing all payments for intangibles is accepted, it will be necessary to add a further section to the income statement. This section would include all of the intangibles expensed during the period and the proceeds of all intangibles sold. It would be desirable, no doubt, for the cumulative effect of all payments and receipts for intangibles to be carried under a special heading in the equity section of the balance sheet. Thus, we would likely end up with a picture somewhat like this:

OWNER'S EQUITY

Contributed Capital		
Common shares	$5,000,000	
Preferred shares	2,000,000	$ 7,000,000
Retained Earnings		
From operations	3,000,000	
Holding gains	1,000,000	4,000,000
		11,000,000
Less: "Intangibles" expensed (net)		2,000,000
		$ 9,000,000

CHAPTER 15

Summing Up

It is surely easy to agree that there is a simple, straightforward way to get better financial statements—just start producing them. We can forget, for the moment, arguments about how much better such statements could be and accept the simple fact that there are many ways presently available to make some improvement. The only essential requirement is that those responsible for publishing statements really want to produce something more informative.

The way to find how far improvements may be carried is first to get things under way, and then find out how far we can proceed before getting stuck. I am convinced that if only we were to initiate an attempt to exploit all the techniques now at our disposal, we would be in for an exciting experience. New techniques and better procedures would be found, and this in turn would stimulate still further developments. But of course, none of this will happen until we kick the habit of worshipping at the altar of the *status quo*. All we have to decide is that we are really going to do what we are supposed to have been doing all along—namely, providing the most useful account we can of what is going on.

The Illogical Base

The trouble is that we have become bogged down in a hopeless attempt to erect a logical structure of principles on an illogical foundation. To someone who wants to know "how a company is doing," cost is interesting when it is a good indication of value. But in cases where cost has ceased to indicate value, who cares about it? Well, some people do—for example, management when faced with a problem which requires project accounting. But for management, or for anyone else who wants a period statement for a complex organization having thousands of projects in various stages of completion (and that's what our published corporate statements are), cost which has ceased to indicate current value cannot have any relevance whatever.

Unrequired Refinements

Our academic types try to help to systematize our approach. But they tend to build elaborate quasi-philosophic or quasi-scientific structures—when what we first need is a simple, reliable base on which to construct usable reports. Polishing and redefining terms is praiseworthy, and no doubt some clarification ensues. But if information is basically misleading—when, for example, you appear to be telling someone what assets and liabilities a company has at a given date, and, mixed in with the information (to an important but unspecified extent), are values which were established years ago, at a time of quite different price levels—then it is hard to believe that it can really matter whether the whole operation is on a rough-and-ready basis or whether the figures have been produced by ingenious mathematical techniques. When we tell someone that the assets are valued at cost less amortization, what advantage is he supposed to derive from knowing this, if it is information in which he cannot possibly be interested? Why bother trying to define such terms as "cost" or "market" more precisely, or to use them more consistently, when no one wants to know what the lower of cost and market value of an inventory is?

The Analogy with Transportation

Groping for a way to sum up all this confusion and frustration, I return to the instructive analogy to which I alluded in Chapter 6—i.e., the analogy between accounting and the transportation industry.

The problem in transportation is the simple and practical one of getting people from one place to another as safely, as expeditiously, and as cheaply as possible. It is the same sort of practical, understandable goal as that which the accountant has in providing useful data to someone who has to make a decision. In both fields, we have operated, over the last couple of centuries, in precisely the same atmosphere of change—and change, moreover, that has gradually accelerated in pace to an almost unendurable crescendo—which is where we are today.

The parallels are actually quite close. Back in the eighteenth century, we were in the stage-coach days, with mud tracks for roads; and at that time, the leading accountants were probably the stewards who devised lists of transactions to apprise the lord of the manor of what was going on. While the roads were gradually being improved, new developments, such as canals and then railways, led to enormous improvements in transportation. At about the same period, a growing interest in joint ventures and the key invention of the limited liability corporation were leading to the development of the balance-sheet concept—and, ultimately, to the articulated balance sheet *cum* income statement which remains, to this day, our basic structure for financial reports.

The parallel can be carried further. The invention of the internal combustion engine led to modern highway trucking and the airplane—in much the same way that punch-card accounting, bookkeeping machines, and control techniques led to greatly improved and speeded-up communication in the financial field. Finally, we are plunged into the age of jet and rocket propulsion—an advance that is closely paralleled by the development of the electronic computer, which is potentially quite as radical an instrument as the interplanetary rocket.

This parallel development was not fortuitous. Progress in transportation required, among other things, better financial data. The awakening interest in railway building meant the organizing of huge ventures, and this contributed to the pressure for better statements. This interdependence continues today, as evidenced by our space program. Exploration of outer space would be impossible without the computer—and would also be impossible without modern tax systems (which rely on accounting at every turn) to support the huge expenditures that are required.

What makes this long parallel development worth stressing is that is demonstrates how, in both fields, changes and improvements come, as it were, at various levels. In the stage-coach days, while coachmen and coach-builders were thinking of improvements such as softer cushions, more reliable lamps, or smoother roads, scientists were working away on research that eventually developed such basic improvements as steam power, internal combustion, and jet propulsion. Similarly, while practical accountants were struggling to make their statement headings less misleading, and to discourage management from creating secret reserves, scientists were working on mechanized and electronic devices that would eventually revolutionize the world of communication.

When I set out on a sort of crusade for better reporting, I had the naïve and overly optimistic notion that the main problem was to persuade accountants that they should find out what statement-users wanted to know—instead of devoting so much ingenuity to devising ways of telling users what accountants thought they should want to know. I thus took every opportunity to ask investors, analysts, bankers, suppliers, and others who use statements, what they would like such statements to tell them. It was a disappointing experience. Apart from the periods of re-crimination which follow, for a brief moment, each recurring financial scandal (during which time everyone is trying, in the interests of his own self-respect, to find someone else to blame for what has happened), statement-users appear to be generally satisfied with the statements which they are getting. They have the notion, I think, that any improvement will introduce complexities which they would rather not hear about. They do make some criticisms. But in my experience, I have found that when invited to be specific, even the serious and well-informed analyst comes up with fairly pedestrian suggestions—a little more information here, some clarification there—but nothing really earth-shaking.

If, at the time, I had thought of the analogy with the transportation business, I would not have been so surprised. Consider the stage-coach days and suppose that a group of forward-looking practitioners (coach-men and coach-builders) were discussing how to improve their per-formance. It might have occurred to some really bright person to suggest that before dreaming up a lot of changes, they should ask their clients— i.e., the passengers—what they would like. If this had happened, imagine the replies! "Some device to keep the draft from the ventilator from blow-ing down the passenger's neck"; "Straw on the floor in winter to prevent frostbite"—that sort of thing, with perhaps some really imaginative type suggesting a grading of steep hills so that passengers would not have to get out and walk up them. If anyone had suggested that the whole con-traption should be made to hurtle through the air at 700 m.p.h. while pretty uniformed girls passed around instant coffee, he would have been locked up in the local loony-bin.

Users get used to using what they are given. Investors who cannot get by with the information available are, I suppose, eliminated by a sort of Darwinian process—through losing the stuff to invest with.

Returning to the stage-coach illustration, we should note that for-tunately, in addition to the enlightened professional operators who were patiently making practical improvements of a tinkering sort, there were a few nuts who were jumping off the barn roof with a set of wildly flapping homemade bamboo wings—with the result that eventually the airplane was invented and developed to a point of commercial feasibility.

The interplay between the coach-builders and the scientists is worth a bit of thought, as it contains a message for us. In accounting, there is the same parallel between those who actually issue statements and try to make practical improvements, and those who seek to refine basic concepts, to develop new data-processing techniques, and to adapt mathematical approaches.

The job of reform, no matter how brilliantly or fervently pursued, will prove endless. Even if we were to reach something which approached perfection, accelerating change would immediately create new problems. An important prerequisite to success is that researchers and practitioners understand each other's position and problems, and, what is perhaps even harder for them to grasp, that they understand their own role and where they themselves can make their contribution.

Transition Period

It stands to reason that if a radical change, such as a full-fledged acceptance of value accounting, is to be adopted, there must be a transition period. General acceptance will not take place overnight. We would therefore face, inescapably, a period in which information in the new form would have to be accompanied by information on the old basis—in order to allow for comparison with the results of other corporations.

One may speculate on the probable length of the transitional period during which a dual accounting would be required. The length of the period would depend on the enthusiasm and vigour with which reforms were pressed. If you want my rough guess, I believe that a complete transition could be made, in such countries as Canada or the United States, in a couple of years under conditions of maximum effort. If the changes were pushed less aggressively, it would, of course, take longer. But the important thing to remember is that no matter how long it takes, if the change is for the better, then we *should* press ahead. Admittedly, the transition period will present some problems—but these will not prove intolerable.

Interim Suggestions

For the pioneers who accept the challenge and adopt changes before they are generally accepted, data on the old basis must be provided at first. This can be done in several ways:

1) *Supplementary data*

The least disturbing procedure (but, from the point of view of reform, also the least satisfactory procedure) is to issue statements in the old form and to provide information in the new form as supplementary data —either in notes to the financial statements or in a report accompanying them. This is better than nothing; but it is still not very good. For one thing, the changes in assets and liabilities do not get worked into the income statement. And secondly, the tendency is for newspaper reports and analysts to pick out only a few figures (notably such popular indices as net earnings per share). Under this system, those who read financial papers or analysts' opinions would tend still to use the old earnings figure—with the result that the valuable new information might easily drop out of sight.

2) *Statements in both forms*

A much better method would be to produce the statements in both forms. The old form could be issued with the customary audit opinion reporting that the statements were prepared in conformity with generally accepted accounting principles. The new form could then be produced with a clear report explaining that the company had issued audited statements in conventional form, but that as conventional reporting is under lively debate, the company had decided, in addition, to issue statements to its shareholders in a form which they might find more enlightening. The nature of the changes and the reasons for them could then be set out. There would not seem to be any likelihood, under these circumstances, that anyone would be misled. If shareholders did not care for the new basis, they could simply ignore it. At least they would not be worse off.

In such cases, it would add to the effectiveness of the new-form statements if the auditors reported on them also. While at first sight it might seem a little startling to suggest that auditors should report on two different sets of statements, and each time give their opinion that the statements present fairly the financial position of the company, this is really not much of a difficulty. After signing a conventional report in the old form, surely it would be proper for the auditors to report on the new form in somewhat the following terms:

> We have examined the accounts of X Co. for the year ended December 31, 1968, and have reported under date of January 30 that the financial statements of the company fairly presented its financial position in accordance with generally accepted accounting principles.
> The attached statements represent an attempt by the company to produce more informative statements. A report accompanying the statements explains the reasons for believing that such statements might be more useful, and the basis on which they have been prepared.

> The attached statements, while not in conformity with generally accepted accounting principles, represent a commendable attempt to overcome some of the weaknesses inherent in the conventional form of statement, and we report that, in our opinion, such statements present fairly the financial position of the company on the basis explained in the report which accompanies them.

The American Accounting Association appointed a committee whose report, entitled *Statement of Basic Accounting Theory*, was issued in August 1966. This excellent report recommended a double-column form of statement showing figures on the conventional basis in one column and figures based on replacement value in the other. The suggestion seemed to be that the former were preferable from the point of view of objectivity, but that the latter were stronger in relevance. Personally, I feel very little enthusiasm for this particular form of uneasy compromise. I believe that it would lead only to confusion if we were to announce a figure for net income of either $2.40 or $3.10 per share—the former figure being somewhat more objectively determined, but the latter being more relevant. For one thing, I don't accept the suggestion that conventional accounting is necessarily more objective than current-value accounting. But, more important still, what is the reader of the statement to conclude? I suppose that in this case he is meant to conclude that earnings are $2.40 a share when calculated on the conventional cost basis, but are $3.10 when "unrealized" gains are taken in (as permitted on the current-value basis). The trouble is, this would be a totally unwarranted conclusion.

Let us examine this case more thoroughly, as it illustrates the outrageous results which can follow from the prevalent tendency to conservatism. The whole object of "cost or lower" is to ensure that net assets and net income are at least not overstated. But the problem is that it doesn't achieve even this irrelevant objective. To begin with, the current-value basis stipulates the inclusion of all liabilities and the immediate recognition of some losses (such as a drop in land values) which need not be taken up under our present rules. Thus, the net-asset position might be lower under current-value accounting than under conventional accounting. But in the typical case, presumably the net-asset position would be higher under current values—so let us take such a case.

While the aim of conventional accounting is to produce statements which show net assets on the low side, there is no way of knowing how much lower than current value these assets are stated. There may indeed be knowledge of certain understatements, but as no overall picture at current value is prepared, there is no way of knowing the overall understatement. It must follow that such understatement will vary from one balance-sheet date to the next. We may illustrate this point with the following figures:

OWNERS' EQUITY

	At current values	Under present conventions
January 1	$800,000	$720,000
December 31	790,000	740,000
Net change	($ 10,000)	$ 20,000

Suppose that a dividend of $25,000 had been paid during the year. The position could be summarized as follows:

	At current values	Under present conventions
Equity at start	$800,000	$720,000
Add: Income	15,000	45,000
	815,000	765,000
Deduct: Dividend	25,000	25,000
Equity at end	$790,000	$740,000

Measuring these results against economic realities, therefore, our so-called conservative accounting would indicate that the dividend was covered almost twice over—whereas in fact it was not even covered once.

This is not a wildly exaggerated illustration, as the "understatement" under present rules is not known and therefore cannot be maintained at a consistent level. Every time it decreases, profits are automatically overstated. You could argue, with good reason, that the chances are that earnings are being overstated under our present endeavours to report profits "on the low, safe side." If this be conservatism, we certainly need another term to describe prudence in financial reporting.

Returning to the AAA committee's recommendation, it seems to me preferable to produce the two forms quite separately, taking plenty of time to explain precisely what we are up to in the new form. The reader can then accept one form or the other, depending on which, in his judgment, will best serve his purpose.

3) *New form with added data*

As a strong critic of conventional statements, I would prefer to go still further and to issue statements officially in the new form with a clear indication of the basis being used. In notes to the statement, data would have to be provided in order to permit the analyst to recast the statements to conventional form should he desire to do so. In such cases, the auditors would report the extent to which the statements failed to comply with generally accepted accounting principles. The reason I like this approach is that it clearly indicates management's preference and, at the same time, maintains that very vital responsibility of management of reporting to the shareholders as fully and as clearly as possible.

4) *New form only*

It is the purpose of this exercise to develop general acceptance of the improved form of presentation. How long this will take depends on how much steam is put behind the effort. When the new form is generally accepted, the old style may be dropped completely.

Taxable Income

It is the tax gatherer's job to "tax the land and find favour in the eyes of the Lord"—and this is not an easy task. Because the tax authorities must treat everyone fairly, they are even more irretrievably attached to general acceptance than the rest of us. It would be absolutely disastrous, therefore, if the tax authorities were encouraged to experiment with new and untried methods. In the transition period which I have been describing, the tax authorities must stick with the older concept of income. But once the new methods have been generally accepted, the tax people will have no real alternative but to switch to the new. They cannot hold out indefinitely on a system of their own for income determination.

In the short run, some of the changes which are advocated in this book will undoubtedly increase the reported income of some companies —and this may seem a very solid argument against the proposals. However, if we go on the reasonable assumption that government will require a certain amount of money to be collected by income taxes (regardless of the gyrations that accountants feel they must go through in preparing financial statements), we must conclude that one of our chief concerns is to have the levy imposed in a manner whereby the required revenue is collected as fairly as possible from the mass of contributors. And as the whole object of current-value accounting is to reflect actual economic realities as closely as possible, it follows, beyond argument, that income taxes based on the proposed method would be fairer than income taxes based on the methods now in fashion. And that surely is all that you can hope to do in devising principles for determining taxable income.

During the transitional period, no tax problem would be presented, since income taxes would continue to be levied on the old basis. We have developed techniques, in recent years, for accounting for deferred taxes when reported income and taxable income are calculated on different bases. While the profession went through much anguish in reaching agreement, we have now established rules to handle this particular problem. In Canada, the CICA handbook lays down the accepted procedures. We may safely conclude, then, that there is no excuse for hiding behind tax problems—since these do not need to enter the picture. The thing to do is to forget about taxes. The changes won't have any effect until the new methods have been generally accepted—and when they have been, we will have a fairer base for tax.

General Conclusions

It is hard to believe that anyone could seriously maintain that our present generally accepted accounting principles constitute a preferable base for financial reporting than current value. Whatever arguments are bandied about in debate, I can think of only two arguments which have any validity: (1) it can be argued that current values cannot be established with sufficient accuracy to be reliable; or (2) it can be argued that financial statements are not taken seriously enough for it to matter what results they report. A word, in conclusion, on each of these points.

Reliability

As has been stated previously, the only way to find out how reliable values can be is to go ahead and produce them—and then see what happens. If, in any situation, no more reliable value than cost can be discovered, then we at least still have cost and are no worse off. We must get down to work at two levels: at the research level, this will mean more fieldwork and less declamation of opinion; and at the statement-production level, it will mean more experimentation. I have been at pains to point out that no grandiose master plan is necessary; in working towards current costs, improvements can be introduced gradually—although I hate to find myself urging caution on my confreres.

In comparison to a slow, piecemeal advance, an overall reform has one tremendous practical advantage which any experienced accountant will appreciate. One of the facts which makes it so hard to get better reporting in practice is that there are so many unrealistic practices condoned by our rules that it becomes very difficult to insist that it is important to take a stand on any one point. Suppose, for example, that an auditor finds that accounts payable are understated by $30,000, and points out that this should be corrected. Just consider the ensuing conversation. It would start something like this:

CLIENT: [Innocently] But why, old boy?

AUDITOR: Because otherwise your income for the period would be overstated by $30,000.

CLIENT: But my reported income is already understated by $50,000 because we have calculated depreciation on out-of-date costs.

AUDITOR: Yes, but that's allowed by generally accepted accounting principles.

CLIENT: Why?

How does the conversation go from this point? Does the auditor say that distortions of income are not objectionable when they arise through faulty depreciation estimates, but are objectionable when they arise from an understatement of liabilities?

The Accounting Principles Board in the United States and the CICA Committee on Accounting and Auditing Research in Canada have both wrestled courageously with the difficult problem of deferred tax accounting, and both have finally emerged with strong statements recommending the proper treatment. (Fortunately, they both agree on what that treatment is!) This is a huge step forward. The auditing profession, in both countries, is showing signs of taking a strong line in support of these pronouncements. The chances are, therefore, that a disastrous diversity of treatment in tax accounting will be avoided. Clearly, however, it makes the problems of taking a courageous stand on any one question much more acute if a recalcitrant statement-issuer can point to other distortions in financial reporting which are sanctioned. Therefore, while I have drawn attention to the possibility of a furtive, creeping approach to reform, the incomparably preferable solution is to do a thorough-going job of it.

The Importance of Financial Data

It may seem ridiculous to have to insist on the fact that high-quality data is necessary. But some people, who should know better, talk as though the balance sheet and income statement are technical productions which can safely be left to the accountants who understand such things. And yet it is these same people who avidly follow return on investment ratios, trends in net earnings per share, and other such popular indices, without seeming to worry that they are all based on technical data in the validity of which they take so little interest.

Ask any investor if he knows what a return on investment ratio is, and he will say, of course, that he does—it is the ratio which indicates how much you are earning on an investment. He will probably go on to explain to you how important it is to watch this indicator—and yet, return on investment ratios cannot be any more realistic than the balance sheets and income statements from which they are produced. In fact, a return on investment ratio could be defined as one way of summarizing the balance sheet and income data.

Someone has calculated that the investment community in the United States is already spending $7,000,000 annually on computerized data banks, from which financial data on important corporations, over a period of years, can be instantly obtained. The basic information for such banks must come from financial statements. It is evident, then, that the statements are considered useful by a vast army of investors and analysts; and when such splendid facilities are available for manipulating and analysing information, it is important that we produce the very best data we can to feed into the system.

Objectivity

My basic proposal involves changing from a system that has worked (at least up to a point) to a value-based accounting which involves a far greater use of value judgments. The importance of such a change can only be appreciated if we recognize, much more clearly than we have tended to do in the past, a basic problem in financial reporting. This is the problem of assuring that those who produce statements do so objectively.

The quality of objectivity is greatly praised, and rightly so. We want financial statements that are prepared fairly—that is, without prejudice. Ideally, those responsible for issuing statements should have no interest in slanting them in any direction—they should let the chips fall where they may. Unfortunately, however, we do not live in a world in which statements can be produced in this way.

It is not sufficiently recognized, I think, that the balance sheet and income account of a corporation are essentially "selling" documents.

In other words, those who produce them have a personal interest in the effect which the statements will produce on those who read them. Let us consider, from this point of view, some of the situations in which the balance sheet and income account are used. These documents are primarily management's reports to shareholders on stewardship. Normally, management will want to be reappointed, and thus must hope that its reports will create a favourable impression of the job that it has been doing. Similarly, when an underwriter or promoter issues a prospectus, he naturally wishes that those who read the prospectus will take a favourable view of the company; and he has, thus, an inescapable interest in the effect which the statements will create. Or again, when the borrower presents his balance sheet to the lender, he hopes that the lender will conclude that it is safe to lend him money. The taxpayer supports his tax return with balance sheet and income account in the hope that the tax authorities will be led to agree with his assessment of tax payable.

In all these cases, those who prepare and issue balance sheets have an interest in the effect which the statements will produce. It might be noted, in passing, that this is not true of all financial statements—there are other statements which can be produced with absolute independence. For example, a company may prepare statements which show how much it would cost to manufacture a certain article, as against how much it would cost to purchase it. If such statements are prepared by an officer of the company who has no interest in which course is chosen, the statements can be completely disinterested. But the balance sheet and income account of commercial corporations cannot be produced in this spirit— and it confuses the whole situation if we do not accept this fact unflinchingly.

It might be thought that statements could be produced independently by a group which is entirely separate from the management of the company. This is perhaps a theoretical possibility—but it is certainly not a practical one. The preparation of statements is so complicated and involves such complete control of the whole data-processing machinery that it would be unthinkable for a group independent of management to attempt the task.

A statutory audit represents one effort to achieve something like independence. A professional firm reports on the annual financial statements, giving an opinion as to whether or not the statements have been properly and fairly prepared. The auditor does, indeed, make a critical examination of the whole statement-producing process—otherwise, he would not be in a position to give a professional opinion. However, his examination is not a completely detailed one. The auditor makes reasonable tests to satisfy himself that the statements present a fair view; but he does so on the understanding that the statements are primarily the responsibility of the corporation. To go further than this would be to extend the auditor's liability to the point where he would have to intervene in the whole operation of the company and control its data processing—an operation, I believe, which anybody who understands the accounting process would recognize as quite impractical.

The statement-producer cannot be unbiased any more than the seller of goods can be unbiased. The analogy with selling should remind us that those who issue statements are not simply confronted with a black and white choice between honesty and dishonesty. There are, in fact, many different shades of bias. For example, presumably no one would suggest that a salesman is not entitled to put his best foot forward. In the simple case of someone who wishes to sell a used car, we would hardly object to the owner's making sure that it was nicely washed and polished. Probably a few touches of paint over rusty areas would not be considered reprehensible. Similarly, some obvious types of repairs might be done, leaving less obvious matters for the purchaser to discover later. Deliberately setting back the speedometer mileage would scarcely be cricket, but is it absolutely necessary to mention that the speedometer was not working for a fair proportion of the vehicle's life?

If we consider the various degrees of "salesmanship" which might be used—from the soft sell to the hard sell—we can easily see that there is no obvious place to draw the line between what is clearly legitimate and what is clearly reprehensible. This is the sort of thing that courts of law try to establish in cases of suspected fraud—and a study of such cases would give some idea of the tremendously laborious process which is involved in investigating any case, and the uncertainty in which decisions of right or wrong must eventually be made. And there is no possibility, amid the multitudinous transactions of the financial world, for a court inquiry into every transaction.

It would, of course, clear up all these difficulties if financial statements could be prepared entirely from objective data—that is, from figures which are produced without value judgments by the accountant. For example, cash receipts and disbursements are historical facts and can be analysed and totalled without value judgments. Undoubtedly, this is how the uninitiated imagine that the accounting process works. However, the hard fact is that sufficiently meaningful figures cannot be compiled in this way. Judgment must be used in producing significant annual reports. As we have seen (in discussing the case of the candid chairman in Chapter 3), *The Accountant*, with its unimpeachable authority, has said flatly that "no one will question the latitude it is possible to exercise in the computation of business profits." This latitude is not permitted through choice. It is unavoidable. We must conclude, therefore, that: (1) a compilation of objective data cannot produce meaningful annual statements; and (2) any usable statement is inevitably subject to possible slanting by those who produce it.

Accountants have tried to steer a course between the horns of this dilemma. They have tried to adhere to a compilation of "facts" where this is possible, and have accepted judgment only where they feel it inevitable. Thus, they have clung to historical cost for fixed assets and have shied away from appraisals, while at the same time writing some asset values down to estimated market—thus producing financial statements which are a hodge-podge of recorded facts and value judgments. As the final overall result is what is most significant, statement-users are left in confusion. They are not aware of the extent to which value judgments have been relied upon; nor are they aware of the extent to which the statements are prepared by a straightforward compilation of statistical facts. Accountants try to help them out with the concept of generally accepted principles—but, as we have seen, these have never been stated (for reasons outlined in Chapter 6) in a clear-cut and satisfactory manner.

We must face frankly the question of whether or not it would be more satisfactory, seeing that statements cannot be entirely factual, to base them entirely on estimated current values. Admittedly, this would introduce more judgment. But if the present compromise statements are subject to manipulation anyway, would it be greatly enlarging the dangers to go whole-heartedly to a value base? A consistent and logical basis for statements would be no more dangerous than the present half-and-half situation and could provide much more useful data when prepared honestly. Producing better statements then, really means facing up to the dilemma outlined above—rather than burying our heads in codes of generally accepted procedure which, in fact, are not generally accepted.

A Combined Operation

It goes without saying that reaching effective general agreement on new principles in the complex business-accounting community will be tremendously difficult—no matter how desirable or logical the new proposals may be. I believe, however, that changes could be made if the various groups concerned with the problem were prepared to work together. Statement reform must be a combined operation which includes the following approaches:

1) *The academics*

Fact-finding research is needed in many areas: investor psychology, valuation techniques, computerization, mathematical approaches, conceptual refinements, etc.

2) *The institutes*

Leadership must continue to be given in the pronouncement area. A huge job is presented by the educative as well as regulatory aspects of institute opinions. To these ends, the institutes must set up committees composed of people who will stop predicting what is likely to happen if certain changes are made, and who will instead be prepared to get down to work and find out what actually *will* happen.

3) *Investment analysts*

What is called for here is a good hard look at the validity of the financial data on which so much analytical work is expended.

4) *Regulatory authorities*

Good communication must be encouraged, and not just misleading information discouraged.

5) *Accountants in public practice*

In their roles both as auditors and advisors to management, professional accountants have a unique opportunity to promote more logical reporting.

6) *Management*

Finally, all members of the management team, whether they have a technical accounting background or not, share the ultimate responsibility for assuring the production of the most useful reports than can be prepared.

*   *   *

To someone who has the strongest doubts about the likelihood of progress by pronouncement and who believes that we will only get by on actual experimentation, it seems a great pity to have to write a book to make the point. But what else can you do when your friends all seem intent on pressing forward up a blind alley?